1 $3 + 1 =$ _____

2 $5 + 1 =$ _____

3 Count up.

1 _____ _____ _____ 5

Count down.

5 _____ _____ _____ 1

4 How much?

_____¢

5 Tom has one ball. He buys one more. How many does he have in all?

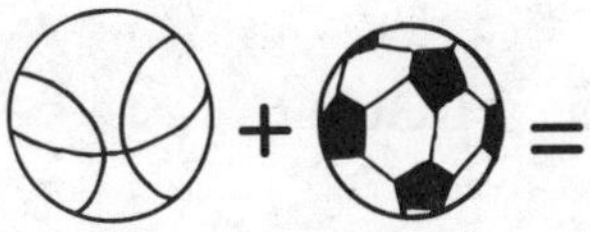

_____ balls

1 $6 + 1 =$ _____

$$\begin{array}{r} 6 \\ +\ 1 \\ \hline \end{array}$$

2 $1 + 7 =$ _____

$$\begin{array}{r} 1 \\ +\ 7 \\ \hline \end{array}$$

3 What is one more than **two**?

- ○ four
- ○ three
- ○ five

4 Color the circles.

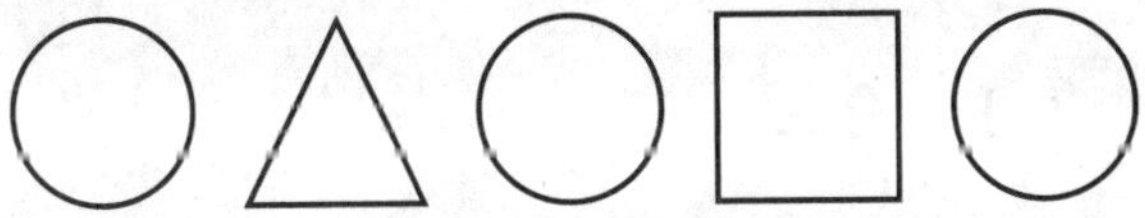

5 Write the numbers.

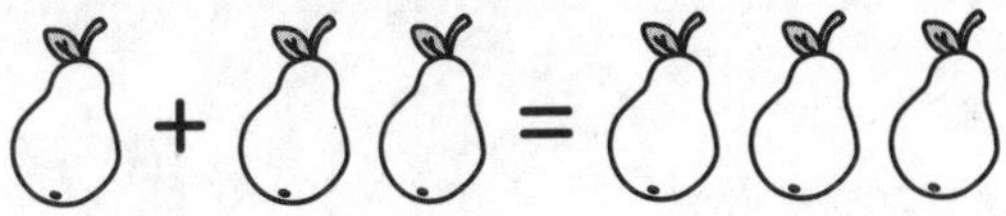

_____ + _____ = _____

I0876932

1. 1 + 4 = _____

2.
```
  1      3
+ 3    + 1
```

3. Sam has two cats and three fish. How many pets does Sam have?

 = ?

_____ pets

4. Add it two ways:

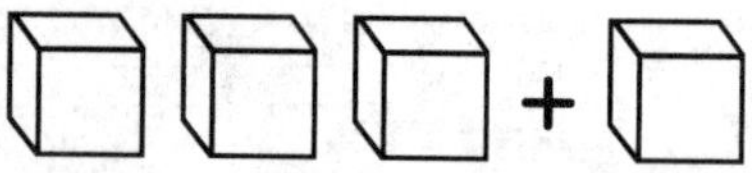 = _____

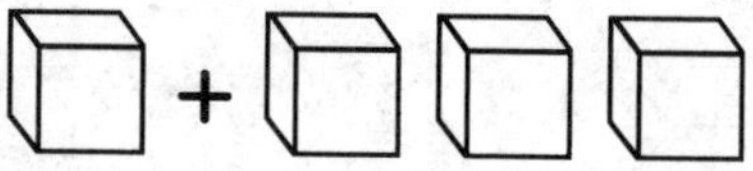 = _____

5. Mark the pattern unit.

- ○ AB
- ○ ABC
- ○ AAB

1. 9 + 1 = _____

   1 + 9 = _____

2. 1 + 2 = _____

3.
```
  8      0
+ 0    + 8
```

4. Circle the numbers.

   4 7 a 9 2 0

   M f 3 5

5. Ann has 1 doll. Tricia has 1 doll. How many dolls are there in all?

   _____ dolls

Activity 1

How many do you have?

 _____ pockets 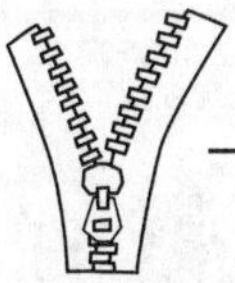 _____ zippers  _____ buttons

Check your answers with a partner.

Activity 2

Circle the pairs. A pair = 2.

WEEK 2 DAY 1 Daily Math Practice

1 Which one is heavier?

2

$$\begin{array}{r}1\\+2\\\hline\end{array}\qquad\begin{array}{r}2\\+2\\\hline\end{array}\qquad\begin{array}{r}3\\+2\\\hline\end{array}$$

3 Color the second one.

first

4

$$\begin{array}{r}4\\+2\\\hline\end{array}\qquad\begin{array}{r}2\\+4\\\hline\end{array}$$

5 How much?

_____ cents

WEEK 2 DAY 2 Daily Math Practice

1 6 + 2 = _____

2 2 + 1 = _____

1 + 2 = _____

3 The bike rack is full. It has four big bikes and two little bikes. How many bikes are there in all?

_____ bikes

4 Are there enough mittens?

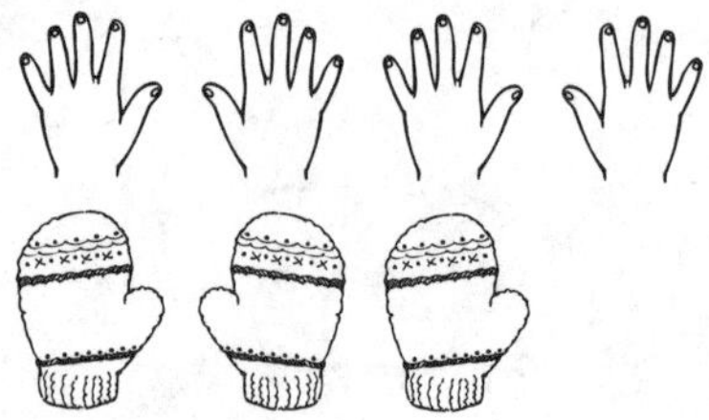

○ **yes** ○ **no**

5 Is this a triangle?

○ **yes** ○ **no**

1. 2 + 7 = ____

2. 3 + 2 = ____

3. Color the ones with four wheels.

4. Write the time.

____ o'clock

5. Write the numbers.

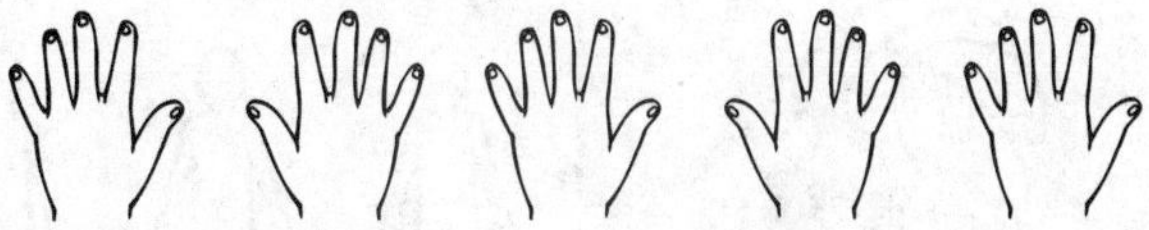

5 10 ____ ____ ____

1. 8 + 2 = ____

2 + 8 = ____

2. 5 + 2 = ____

3. Write the numbers.

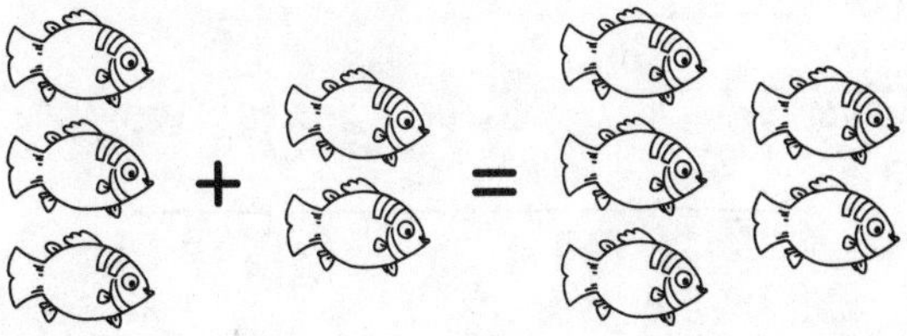

____ + ____ = ____

4. Mrs. Brown has two new pairs of shoes. How many new shoes does she have in all?

____ shoes

5. What comes next?

△ △ ○ △ △ ____

Look at the graph. Then answer the questions. 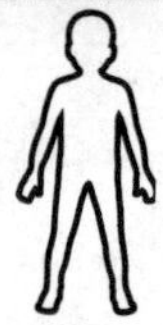 = **1 child**

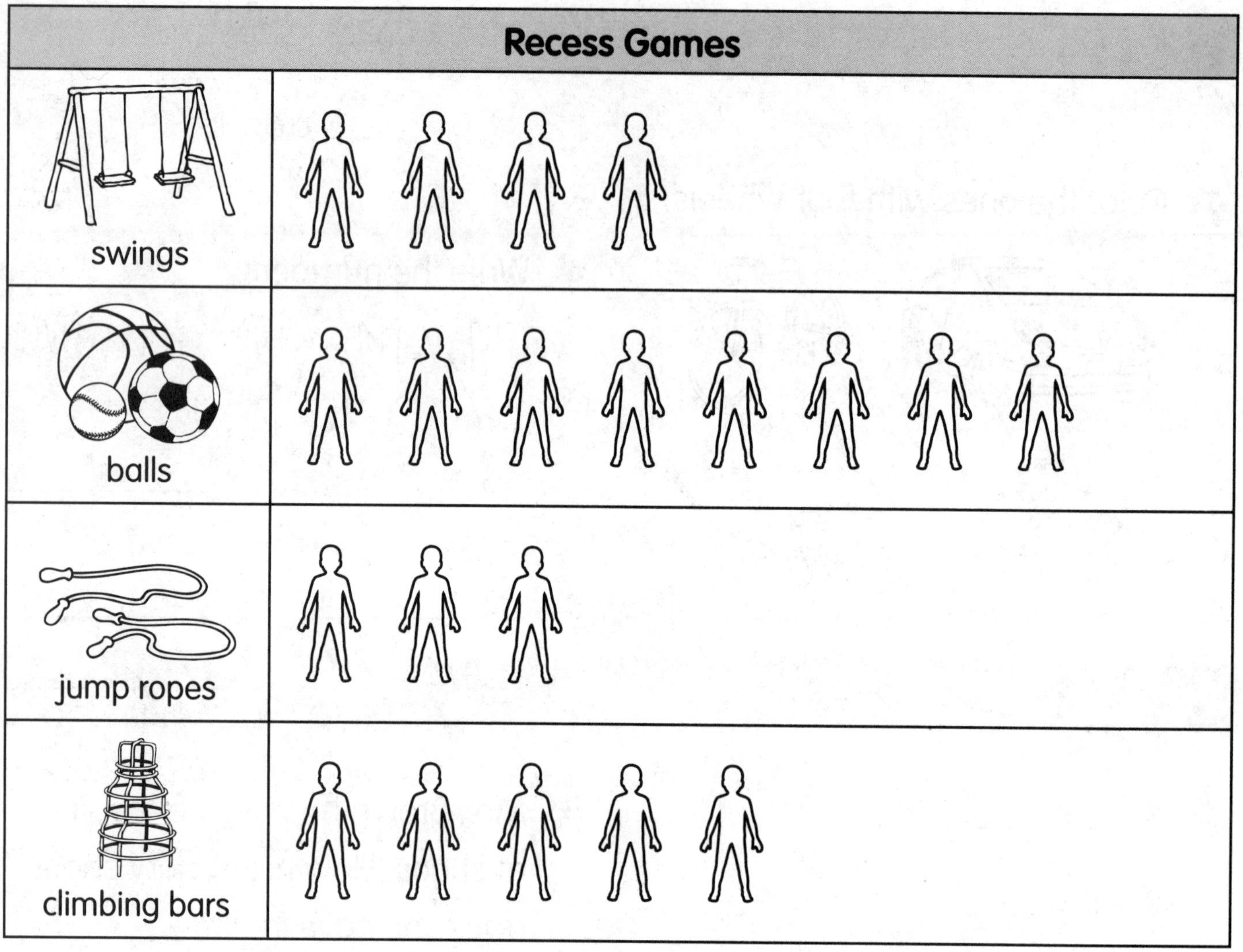

1. How many children played each game?

   swings _____ jump ropes _____

   balls _____ climbing bars _____

2. Which game did the most children play? _______________

1. 3 + 5 = ____

2. 4 + 3 = ____

   3 + 4 = ____

3. Write the number.

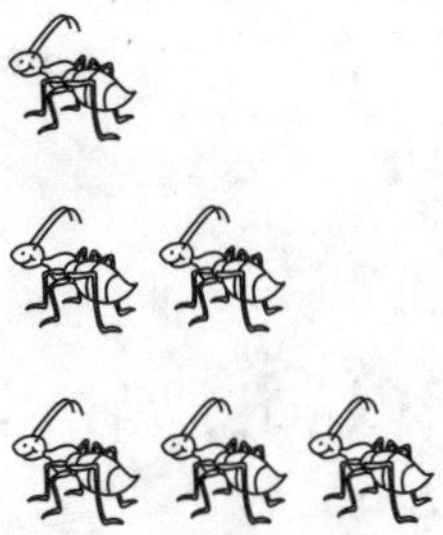

one ____

two ____

three ____

4. Write = in the box if they are the same.

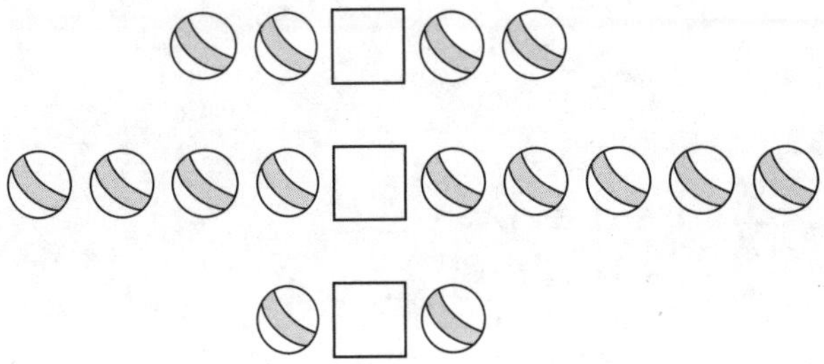

5. The dog had one bone. He found three more bones. How many bones did he have in all?

____ bones

1.

$$\begin{array}{r} 2 \\ +\,2 \\ \hline \end{array} \qquad \begin{array}{r} 3 \\ +\,3 \\ \hline \end{array} \qquad \begin{array}{r} 4 \\ +\,4 \\ \hline \end{array}$$

2.

$$\begin{array}{r} 7 \\ +\,3 \\ \hline \end{array} \qquad \begin{array}{r} 6 \\ +\,4 \\ \hline \end{array} \qquad \begin{array}{r} 5 \\ +\,5 \\ \hline \end{array}$$

3. Mia had five cookies. She ate one. How many were left?

____ cookies

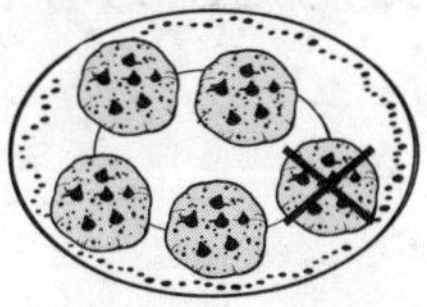

4. How many?

sides ____

corners ____

5. Write the numbers.

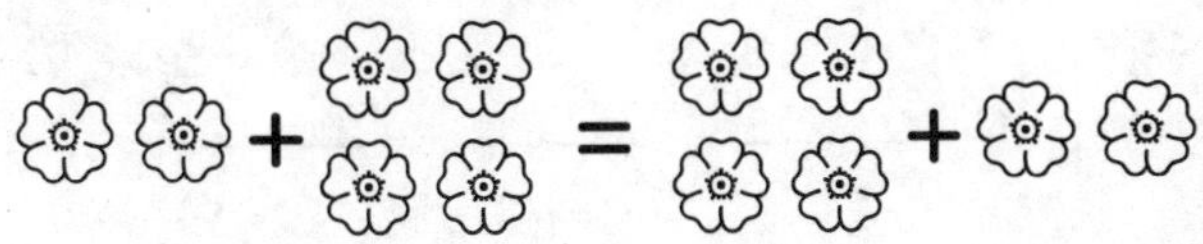

____ + ____ = ____ + ____

1. $2 + 3 =$ ____

   $3 + 2 =$ ____

2. $1 + 1 + 1 =$ ____

3. About how many eggs?

2 12 100

4. Two birds were in the nest. One flew away. How many were left?

   ____ bird

5. How many fingers?

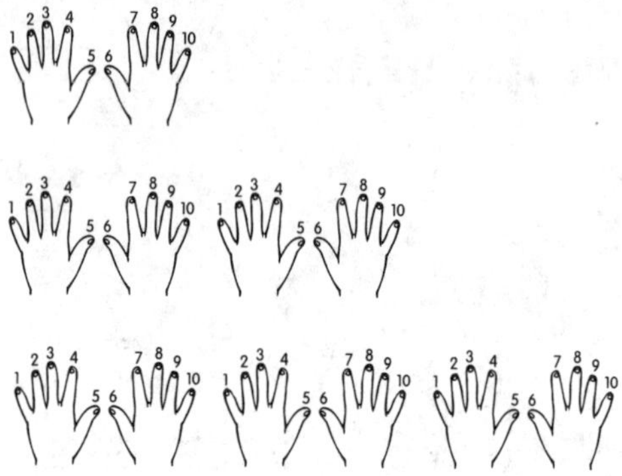

____

____

____

1. $\begin{array}{r} 3 \\ +\ 8 \\ \hline \end{array}$ $\begin{array}{r} 8 \\ +\ 3 \\ \hline \end{array}$

2. Write the numbers.

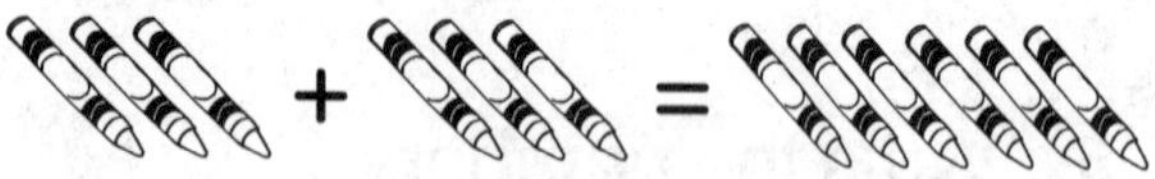

____ + ____ = ____

3. Color $\frac{1}{2}$ of the ball.

4. How many?

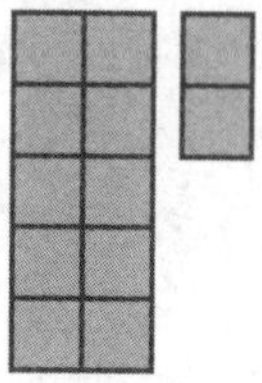

____ ten + ____ ones = ____

5. The train has a , a , and two . How many cars does it have in all?

   ____ cars

1. What comes next?

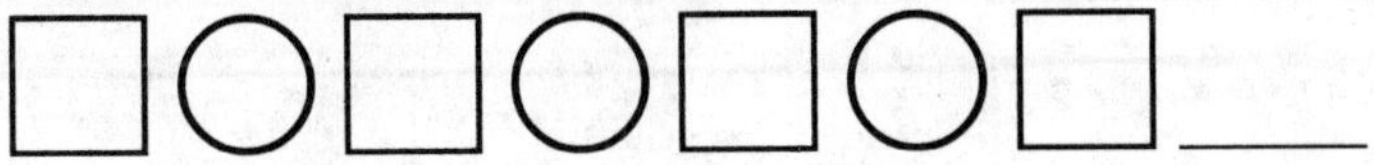

Mark the pattern unit.

○ ABB ○ AB ○ ABCC

2. Color an AAB pattern.

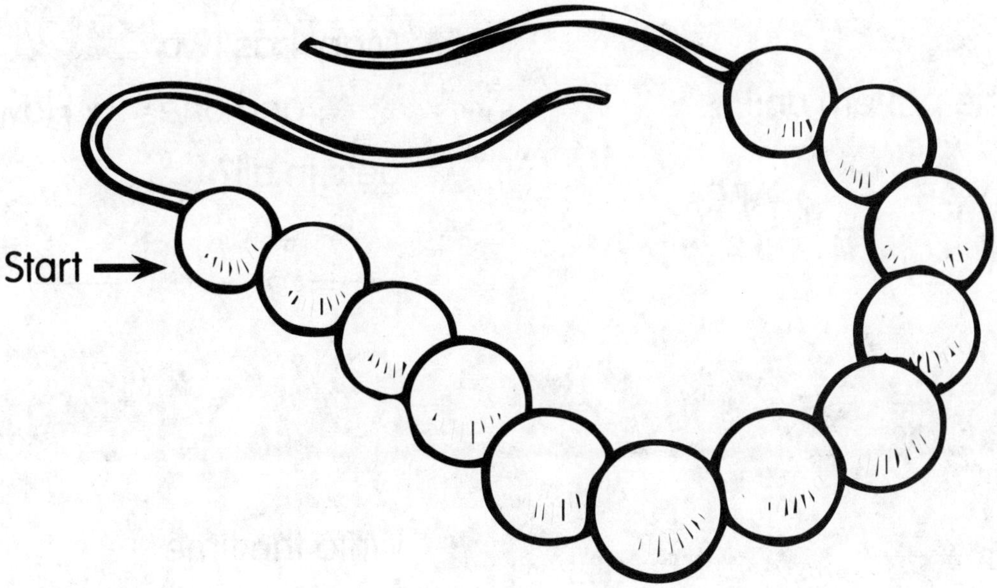

3. Draw an ABCC pattern.

1 4 + 5 = ____

2 2 + 4 = ____

3 What comes next?

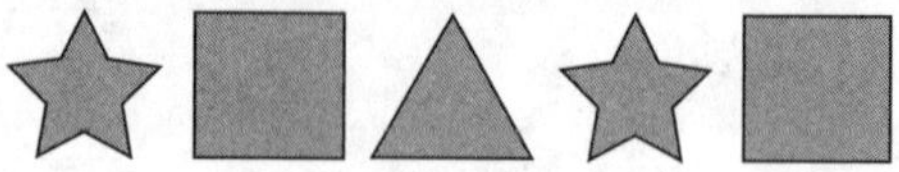 ____

Mark the pattern unit.

○ AB ○ ABC

4 Make one tally for each flower.

	|
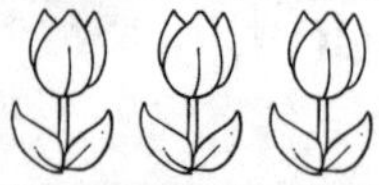	

5 Mary has two , one , and one . How many pets in all?

____ + ____ + ____ = ____

1 4 + 4 = ____

5 + 5 = ____

2 4 + 6 = ____

3 Kai has one little , two little , three little . How many kittens does he have in all?

____ kittens

4 Write the time.

____ o'clock

5 Write the number.

six ____ eight ____

seven ____ nine ____

WEEK 4 DAY 3 Daily Math Practice

1 4 + 3 = _____

2 4 + 7 = _____

3 Color the square blue.
Color the circle red.
Color the triangle yellow.

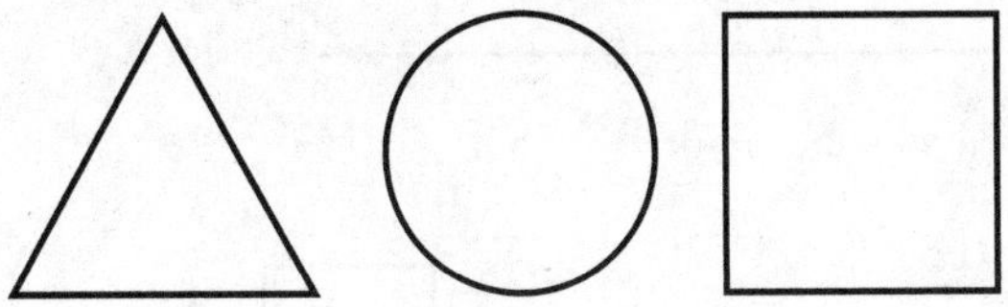

4 Bob put two cherries in the bowl.

0 + 2 = _____

Bob ate two cherries.

2 – 2 = _____

5 Luis has two green hats and three red hats. How many hats does he have in all?

_____ hats

WEEK 4 DAY 4 Daily Math Practice

1 1 + 8 = _____

2

8	7	6
+ 4	+ 4	+ 4
___	___	___

3 Rita has four big beads and two little beads. How many beads does she have in all?

_____ beads

4 Write the numbers.

_____ + _____ = _____

5

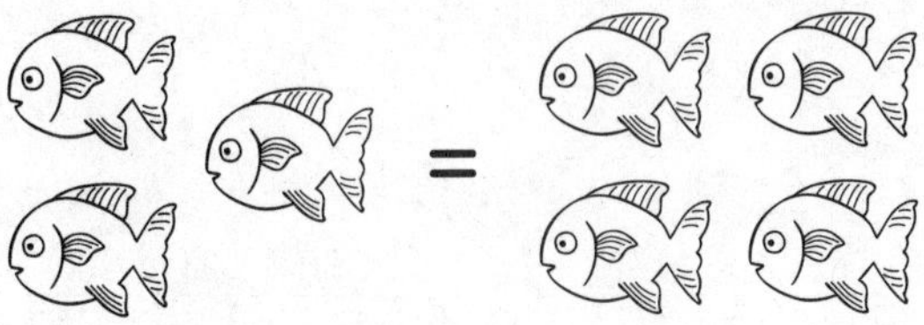

○ **yes** ○ **no**

1. You will color the shapes to sort them into two groups.

Color the shapes with 3 sides red.

Color the shapes with 4 sides blue.

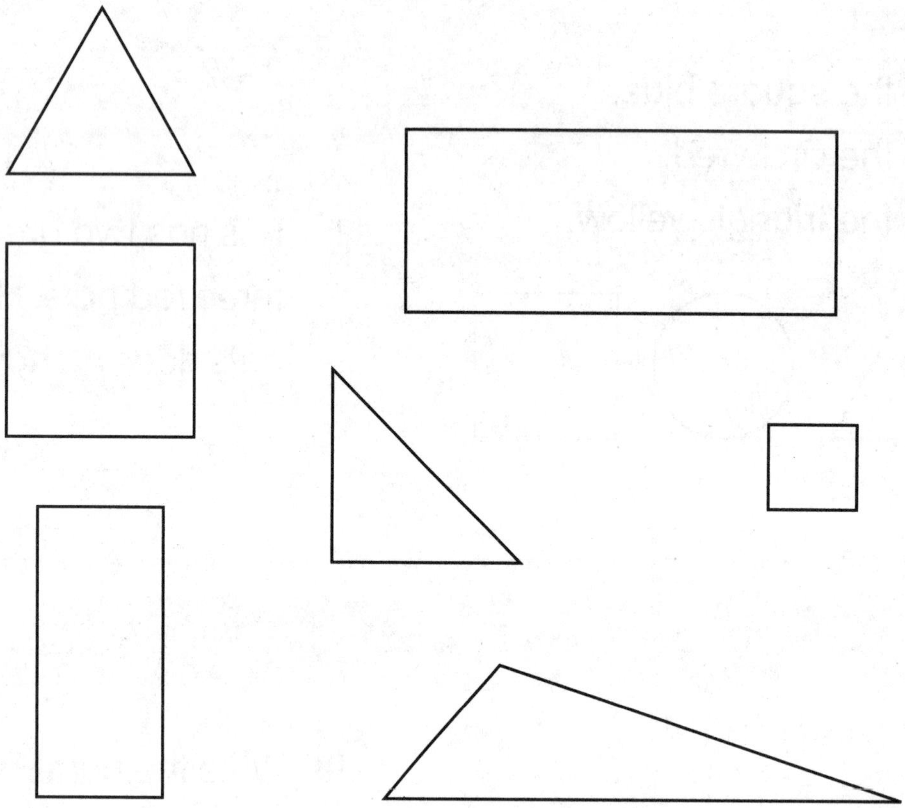

2. The red group has ____. ○ squares ○ triangles

3. The blue group has squares and triangles. ○ **yes** ○ **no**

1. 5 − 1 = _____

2. 7 − 1 = _____

3. What is 3 + 3? _____

   What is 4 + 4? _____

   What is 5 + 5? _____

4. How much?

_____ cents

5. How many stamps?

_____ stamps

1. 2 + 4 = _____

2. 10 − 1 = _____

   1 + _____ = 10

3. Count down.

   10 _____ _____ _____ _____ _____

   _____ _____ _____ _____ 0

4. 3 + 2 = 5 ○ **yes** ○ **no**

   2 + 3 = 5 ○ **yes** ○ **no**

   5 + 2 = 3 ○ **yes** ○ **no**

5. Sally ate two carrots, one apple, and four grapes. How many things did she eat?

   _____ things

1 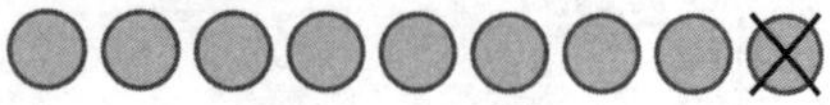

9 – 1 = ____

2 5 + 5 = ____ 4 + 4 = ____

3 + 3 = ____ 2 + 2 = ____

3 There were ten cats in the bed, and one rolled out. How many were left?

____ cats

4 Mark the pattern unit.

○ AB ○ AAB

What shape comes next? ______

5 Write the numbers.

 + 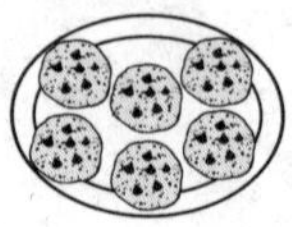 = ?

____ + ____ = ____

1 10 11 12 ____ ____ ____ 16

2 4 – 2 = ____

3 Mr. Black has five fish.
Mr. Brown has seven fish.
Who has more fish?

○ Mr. Black ○ Mr. Brown

4 $\begin{array}{r} 6 \\ -\ 1 \\ \hline \square \end{array}$ $\begin{array}{r} \square \\ +\ 1 \\ \hline 6 \end{array}$

5 4 + 0 = 4 ○ **yes** ○ **no**

0 + 4 = 4 ○ **yes** ○ **no**

4 + 4 = 0 ○ **yes** ○ **no**

1. Number the balls in order from smallest to largest.

___ 1 ___ ___ ___ ___

2. Number the dogs in order from largest to smallest.

___ 1 ___ ___ ___

1. 5 – 2 = _____

2. 4 + 3 = _____

   5 + 3 = _____

3. Mark has two pennies. His mom gives him three more pennies. How many pennies does he have in all?

   _____ pennies

4. What time is it?

○ 1 o'clock
○ 10 o'clock
○ 11 o'clock

5. Circle the third hat.

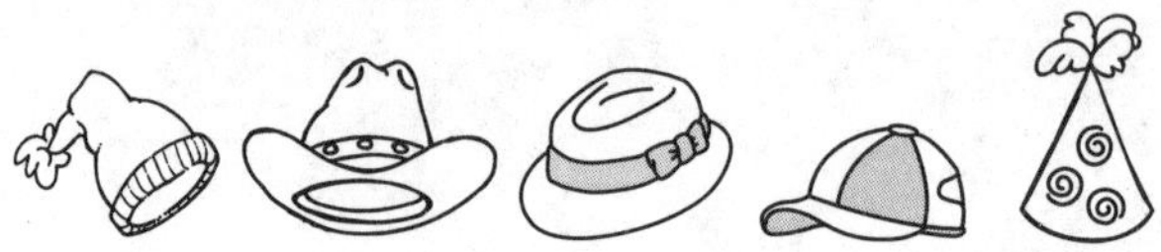

1. 8 – 2 = _____

2. 2 – 2 = _____

3. Draw a triangle.

   How many sides? _____

   How many corners? _____

4. Which is heavier? Circle it.

5. Sean has three letters to mail. He needs a stamp for each letter. How many stamps does he need?

   _____ stamps

1 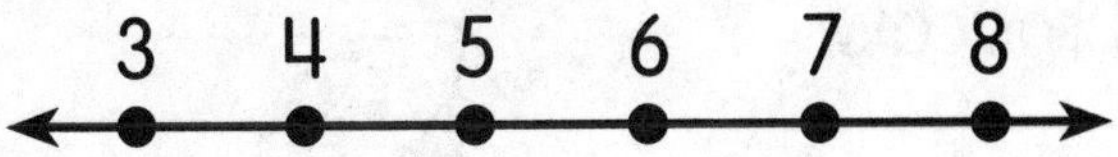

7 – 2 = ____

2 5 + 3 = ____

3 How many petals?

 5

 ____

 ____

 ____

4 Mark the square buttons that have two holes.

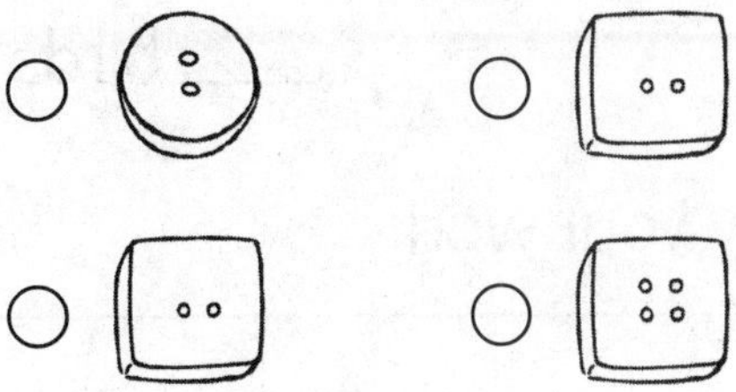

5 There were two red fish and five blue fish. How many fish were there in all?

____ fish

1 6 – 2 = ____

6 – 4 = ____

2 4 + 5 = ____

3 Ron read six pages yesterday and four pages today. How many more pages did he read yesterday?

____ more pages

4 Mark the number sentence that tells about the picture.

○ 3 + 2 = 6

○ 3 + 2 = 5

○ 3 – 2 = 5

5 3 + 1 – 1 = ____

1. Jack has 3 parrots, 2 parakeets, and 1 macaw. How many birds does he have in all?

_____ birds

Show your work.

2. If Jack can keep 2 birds in a cage, how many cages does he need?

_____ cages

Show your work.

1 

5 – 3 = _____

2 4 + 6 = _____

3 + 6 = _____

3 There were six eggs in the box. Two eggs broke. How many are left?

_____ eggs

4 Which is $\frac{1}{2}$?

○ 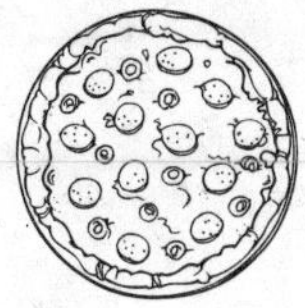 ○ 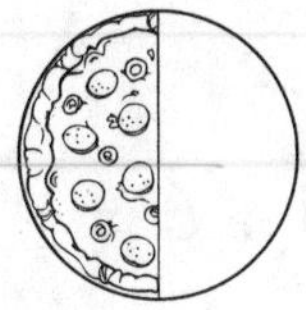

5 Write a story problem for

6 + 1 = ?

____

____

____

1 8 – 3 = _____

2 4 + 3 = _____

3 + 4 = _____

3 5 = 5 ○ **yes** ○ **no**

5 = 6 ○ **yes** ○ **no**

5 = 4 ○ **yes** ○ **no**

4 What comes next?

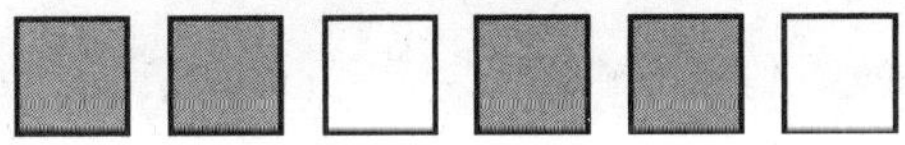 _____

5 There are two red beads, two blue beads, and two green beads. How many beads are there in all?

_____ beads

1 3 – 3 = _____

2 1 + 6 = _____

6 + 1 = _____

3 About how many potatoes?

○ 5 ○ 20 ○ 200

4 4 + 2 = 2 + 4 ○ **yes** ○ **no**

5 + 2 = 2 + 4 ○ **yes** ○ **no**

5 Write a number sentence to tell how many.

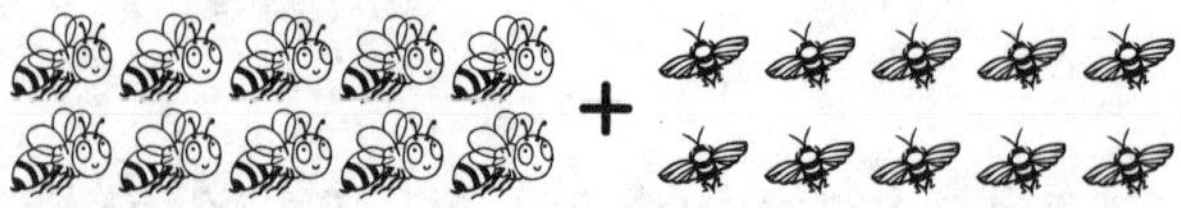

____

1 

9 – _____ = _____

2 6 + 3 = _____

3 Write the number.

ten _____

five _____

seven _____

4 Color the squares.

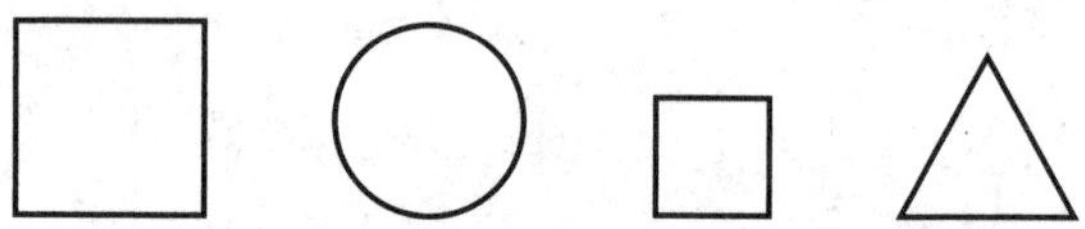

5 Tommy found three big feathers and three little feathers. How many feathers did he find in all?

_____ feathers

Mrs. Watson's class made a weather graph. Look at the graph to answer the questions.

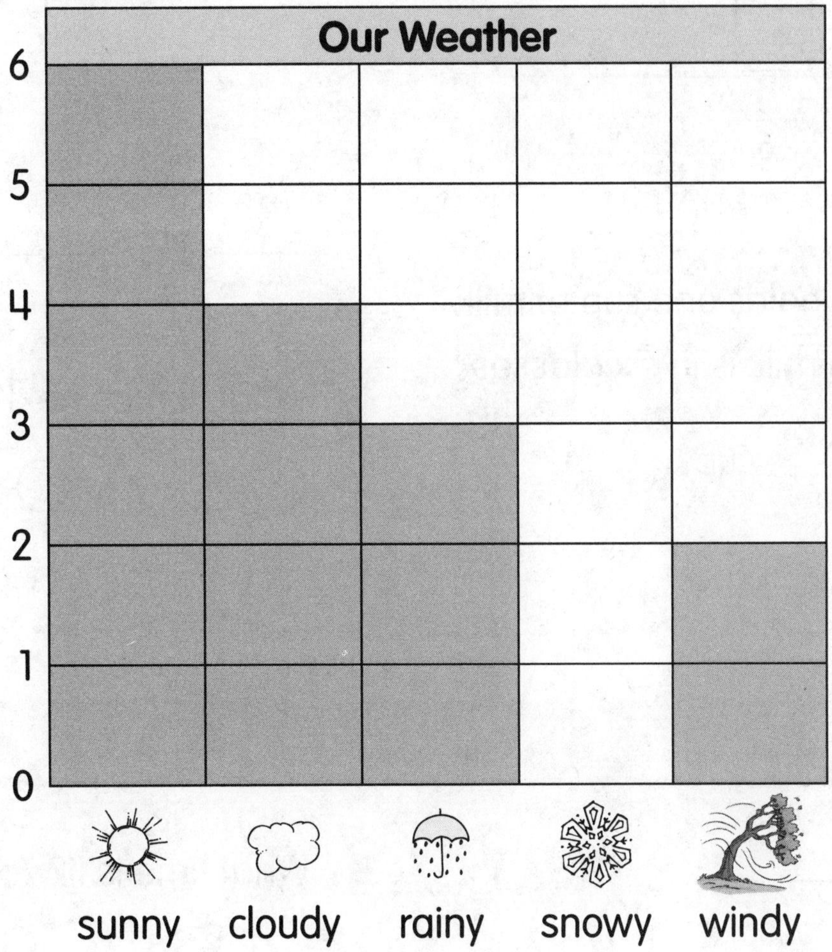

1. How many rainy days? _____

2. How many cloudy days? _____

3. Were there more rainy and cloudy days together than sunny days?

   ○ **yes** ○ **no**

4. Write something else you know from the graph.

____

WEEK 8 DAY 1 Daily Math Practice

1. 3 + 7 = _____

2.
```
  6        □
- 4      + 4
---      ---
  □        6
```

3. Each glass holds one cup of milk. How much milk is in six glasses?

   _____ cups

4.

ten	ones

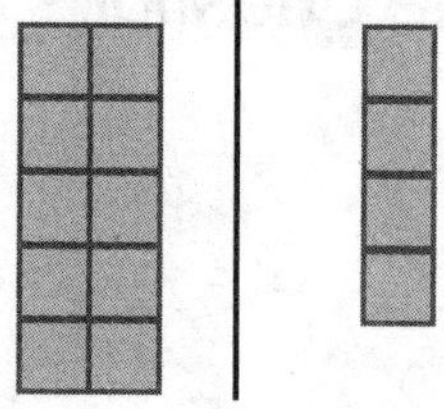

_____ ten + _____ ones = _____

5. What comes next?

   ○ △ △ ○ △ _____ _____

WEEK 8 DAY 2 Daily Math Practice

1. 8 – 4 = _____

2.
```
  6        3
+ 3      + 6
---      ---
```

3. There are five frogs on a log. If two frogs jump off, how many will be left?

   _____ frogs

4. What time is it?

○ 12:00
○ 9:00
○ 9:30

5. Write the numbers.

   two + three + four = nine

   _____ + _____ + _____ = _____

1. 10 + 10 = _____

2.
```
  9      4
– 4    + 9
___    ___
```

3. Five boys and five girls went on a hike. How many children hiked in all?

   _____ children

4. Count by twos.

_____ _____ _____ _____ _____

5. $4 < 4$ ○ yes ○ no

   $4 > 4$ ○ yes ○ no

   $4 = 4$ ○ yes ○ no

1. 7 – 4 = _____

2. 10 – 5 = _____

3. There were 25 students in Mrs. White's class. Then 1 new student came. How many are in Mrs. White's class now?

   _____ students

4. Color the triangles.

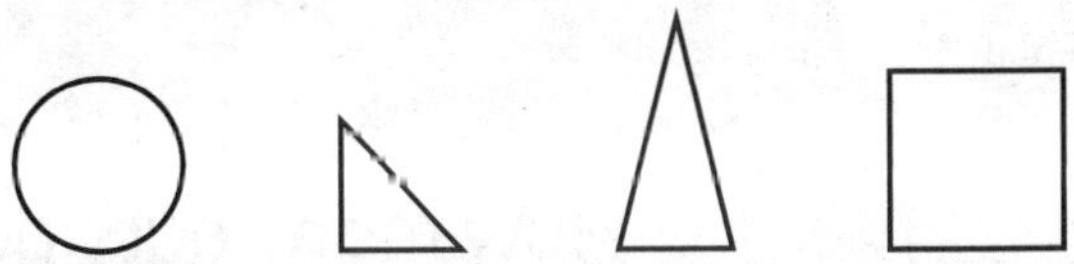

5. Write a number sentence.

_____ + _____ = _____

➤ Activity 1

Count from **1** to **50**.

	2			5					10
11					16				20
		23						29	
	32			35					
41						47			50

➤ Activity 2

Answer the questions.

How many ears do six elephants have? _____ ears

How many feet do four zebras have? _____ feet

How many tails do three monkeys have? _____ tails

1. $9 - 5 =$ _____

2. $4 + 6 =$ _____

   $6 + 4 =$ _____

3. Wes has two bags of candy. Each bag has 6 pieces. How much candy does Wes have in all?

   _____ pieces

4. Are the teams equal?

   ○ **yes** ○ **no**

5. How much?

   _____ cents

1. $8 - 5 =$ _____

2. $\begin{array}{r} 4 \\ +\,5 \\ \hline \square \end{array}$ $\qquad$ $\begin{array}{r} \square \\ -\,4 \\ \hline 5 \end{array}$

3. There are five eggs in a nest. If one egg breaks, how many will be left?

   _____ eggs

4. Count back.

   20 19 18 _____ _____

   _____ _____ _____ _____

5. How many tens?

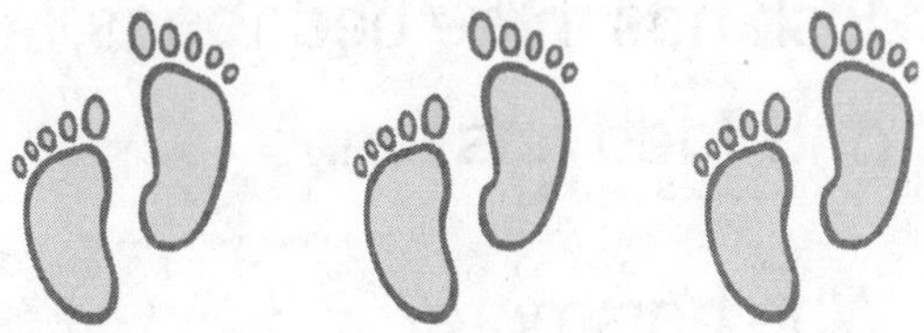

   _____ tens

WEEK 9 DAY 3 Daily Math Practice

1 3 + 3 + 2 = ____

2 9 – 6 = ____

10 – 6 = ____

3 Maria's coat has 4 buttons in the front and 2 on each sleeve. How many buttons does Maria's coat have in all?

____ buttons

4 3 + 4 = 7 ○ **yes** ○ **no**

4 – 7 = 3 ○ **yes** ○ **no**

4 + 3 = 7 ○ **yes** ○ **no**

7 – 3 = 4 ○ **yes** ○ **no**

5 A square has three equal sides.

○ **yes** ○ **no**

Draw a square.

WEEK 9 DAY 4 Daily Math Practice

1 10 – 4 = ____

2 7 + 2 = ____

____ – 7 = 2

3 Josh has three beanbags, and Todd has four.

Who has more? ________

How many more? ____

4 Mark the pattern unit.

○ AB ○ AAB ○ ABB

5 What comes next?

19 20 21 ____

47 48 49 ____

➤ Activity 1

Write your name in two different patterns.

Examples:

Pattern:	PEtePEtePEte	PeTePeTePeTe
Pattern Unit:	AABB	AB

Name the pattern unit. ________

Name the pattern unit. ________

➤ Activity 2

Write the missing numbers.

10 20 30 ____ ____ 60 ____ ____ ____ ____ ____

5 10 15 ____ 25 ____ ____ ____ ____ ____ ____

2 4 6 ____ 10 12 ____ ____ ____ ____ ____ ____

1 $12 - 2 =$ ____

2 $\begin{array}{r} 5 \\ 3 \\ +\,1 \\ \hline \end{array}$ $\qquad$ $\begin{array}{r} 5 \\ +\,4 \\ \hline \end{array}$

3 The apple tree had six apples. Bob picked two. How many apples were left?

____ apples

4 Color the fifth duck.

5 $4 + 2 = 6$ ◯ **yes** ◯ **no**

$3 + 3 = 6$ ◯ **yes** ◯ **no**

$6 + 0 = 6$ ◯ **yes** ◯ **no**

$5 + 2 = 6$ ◯ **yes** ◯ **no**

1 $10 - 7 =$ ____

$11 - 7 =$ ____

2 $8 + 3 =$ ____

3 Jenny picked up two pennies. She put them with her other six pennies. How many pennies does Jenny have now?

____ pennies

4 Circle the hats that have stripes and bills.

5 Write the time.

____ o'clock

1 $5 + 2 + 4 =$ _____

2 What number is one less?

_____ 13

_____ 26

3 Sue had a double scoop of ice cream. Tom had a triple scoop. Who had the smallest amount?

○ Sue ○ Tom

4 How many?

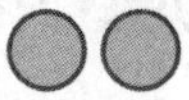 = _____ 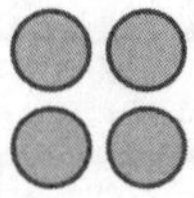 = _____

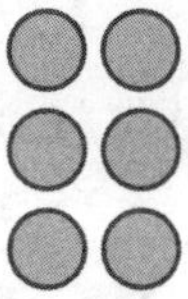 = _____ 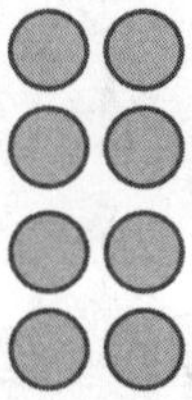 = _____

5 Which weighs more?

○  ○ 

1 $9 - 8 =$ _____

$12 - 11 =$ _____

2 $9 + 7 =$ _____

3 Tommy had 10 cents. He bought a pencil for 5 cents. How much does he have left?

_____ cents

4 Color the squares.

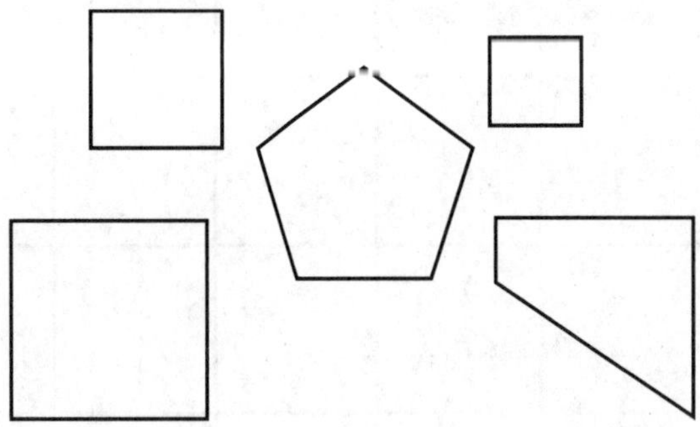

5 Four cherries and five grapes

equal _____ pieces of fruit.

➤ Activity 1

Use the number line to solve the problem.

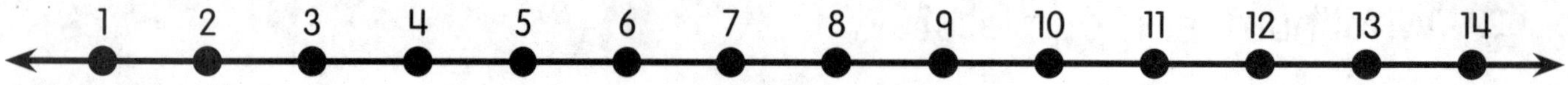

10 – 5 + 6 – 1 + 4 – 2 = _____

Show your work here.

➤ Activity 2

Count from **51** to **110**.

51	52	53							60
					66		68		
71			74						80
				85					
								99	
101	102	103				107			110

WEEK 11 DAY 1 Daily Math Practice

1. $5 + 5 =$ _____

   $5 + 4 =$ _____

2. $12 - 2 =$ _____

3. Juan's family ate four tortillas for lunch and four tortillas for dinner. How many did they eat in all?

   _____ tortillas

4. Write the number.

   eight _____

   four _____

   twelve _____

   zero _____

5. $2 + 2 + 2 + 2 =$ _____

   $10 + 10 + 10 + 10 =$ _____

WEEK 11 DAY 2 Daily Math Practice

1. $8 + 3 =$ _____

   _____ $- 8 = 3$

2. $3 + 2 + 3 =$ _____

3. I saw six sea stars, three snails, and a sunfish at the beach. How many animals did I see?

   _____ animals

4. Color $\frac{1}{2}$. Color 1 whole.

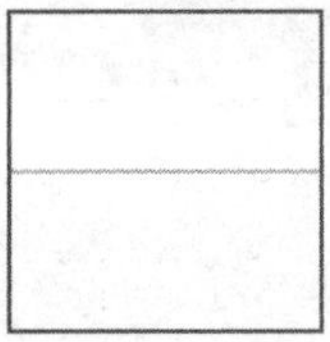

5. $5 + 4 = 4 + 5$

   ○ **yes** ○ **no**

   $6 + 4 = 4 + 5$

   ○ **yes** ○ **no**

WEEK 11 DAY 3 Daily Math Practice

1. 10 + 9 = _____

   _____ – 10 = 9

2. 2 + 6 = _____

3. 10 = 5 + 4 ○ **yes** ○ **no**

   10 < 5 + 4 ○ **yes** ○ **no**

   10 > 5 + 4 ○ **yes** ○ **no**

4. Draw three circles.

   Color one blue. Color two red.

   Write a number sentence to tell about the circles.

   _____ + _____ = _____

5. 5 boys + 5 girls + 1 dog = _____

WEEK 11 DAY 4 Daily Math Practice

1. 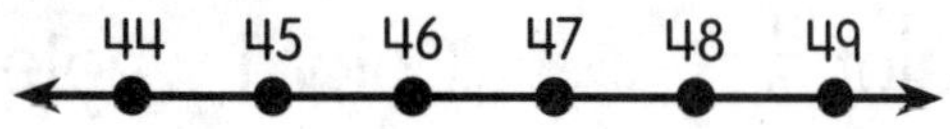

   45 + 3 = _____

2. 

   17 – 5 = _____

3. Three girls each have three bears. How many bears do they have in all?

   _____ bears

4. About how many crayons?

   ○ almost 6

   ○ almost 20

   ○ almost 160

5. Write four number sentences using **4**, **2**, and **6**.

   _____ + _____ = _____

   _____ + _____ = _____

   _____ – _____ = _____

   _____ – _____ = _____

For nine months, the students in Mrs. Timm's class put a 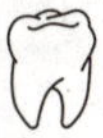 on a graph every time one of them lost a tooth. Look at the graph to answer the questions.

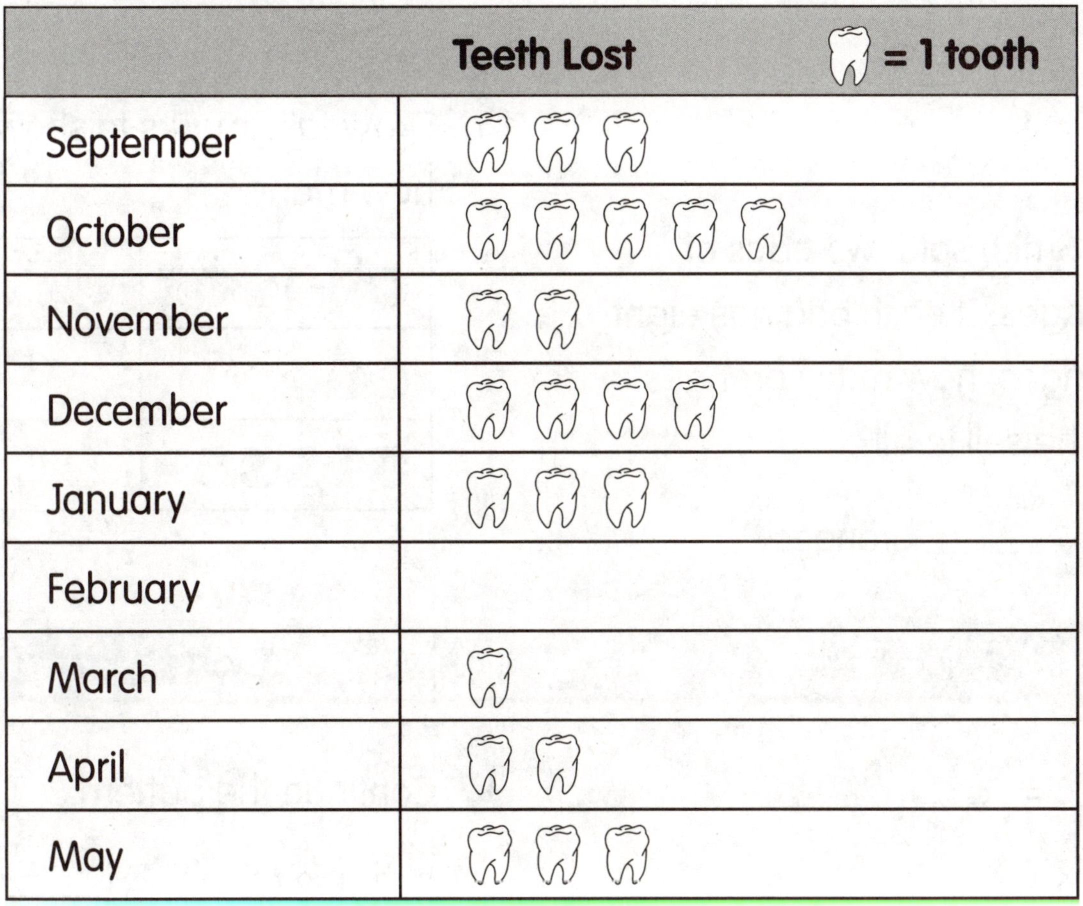

1. How many teeth have been lost in all? _____ teeth

2. In which month were the most teeth lost?

   ○ February ○ October ○ May

3. In which month were the fewest teeth lost?

   ○ March ○ September ○ February

1.
```
  4      14
+ 3     + 3
```

2.
```
  7       7
- 4     - 3
```

3. Mr. Smith sold two bags of oranges. If each bag has eight oranges, how many oranges did he sell in all?

_____ oranges

4. Write the time.

_____ o'clock

5. Draw tally marks to show how many.

1. 6 + 6 = _____

6 + 6 + 6 = _____

2. 30 + 20 = _____

3. There are two raisins on each cookie. How many raisins are there on three cookies?

_____ raisins

4. Continue the pattern.

2 2 1 2 2 1 _____ _____ _____

_____ _____ _____

5. Count the eyes.

_____ _____ _____ _____

WEEK 12 DAY 3 Daily Math Practice

1 How many?

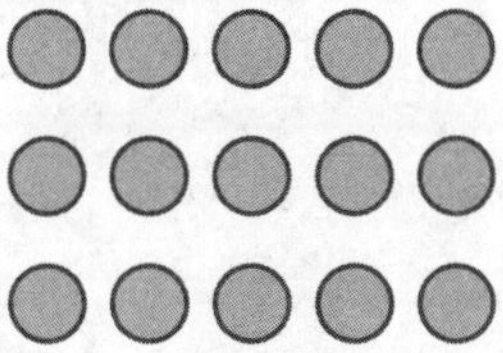

= _____

2 54 + 1 = _____

3 There are two peanuts in each shell. How many peanuts are in six shells?

_____ peanuts

4 Draw an **X** on the spheres.

5 Add two.

5 + 2 = _____

Then subtract two.

_____ − 2 = _____

WEEK 12 DAY 4 Daily Math Practice

1 4 + 3 + 2 + 1 = _____

2 13 − 7 = _____

7 + _____ = 13

3 Jose read two books every day. How many books did he read in five days?

_____ books

4 Write the number.

thirty-six

twenty-seven _____

5 Draw an **X** on $\frac{1}{4}$.

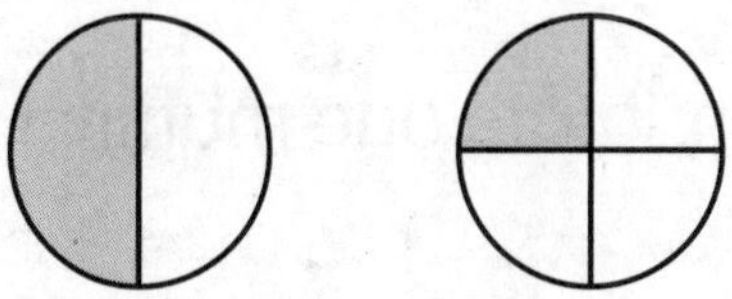

Sienna went to the store to buy snacks. She bought four muffins, six oranges, and five carrots. Draw the snacks on the chart.

muffins 	oranges 	carrots 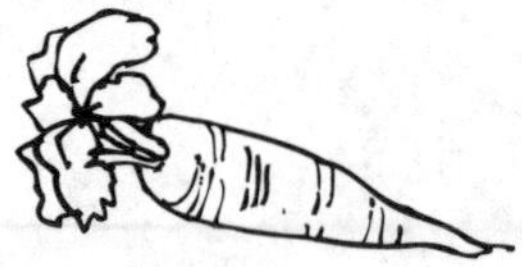

Use the chart to answer the questions.

1. How many snacks did Sienna buy in all?

_____ + _____ + _____ = _____ snacks

2. Sienna ate one muffin. How many snacks does she have now?

_____ – _____ = _____ snacks left

1 How many?

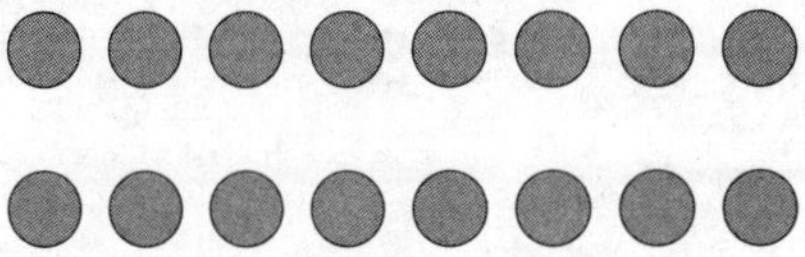

= _____

2 20 – 10 = _____

3 Carl rode his bike two blocks to the park and two blocks home. How far did he ride?

_____ blocks

4 Which pattern is shown below?

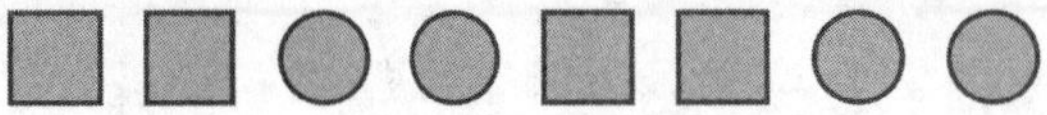

○ ABA ○ AABB ○ ABBA

5 How much?

_____ cents

1 0 + 15 = 7 + 8

○ **yes** ○ **no**

2 2 + 9 = _____

3

$$\begin{array}{r} 3 \\ +\ 4 \\ \hline \square \end{array} \qquad \begin{array}{r} \square \\ -\ 3 \\ \hline 4 \end{array}$$

4 Draw an **X** on the circles.

5 Brett and Bonnie ate pizza for lunch. They each had four pieces. How many pieces did they eat in all?

_____ pieces

WEEK 13 DAY 3 Daily Math Practice

1. 6 + 4 = ____

   7 + 3 = ____

2. 14 – 13 = ____

3. 1 + 15 = 16 ○ **yes** ○ **no**

   15 + 1 = 16 ○ **yes** ○ **no**

   16 + 1 = 15 ○ **yes** ○ **no**

4. Write a story problem about birds for **5 – 2 = 3**.

   ____

   ____

   ____

   ____

5. How much?

   = ____¢

WEEK 13 DAY 4 Daily Math Practice

1. $6 + 4 < 7 + 7$

   ○ **yes** ○ **no**

2. 14 – 2 = ____

3. Seline put three cookies and two brownies in a box for her grandma. How many treats will her grandma have altogether?

   ____ treats

4. Circle **odd** or **even**.

 **odd** **even**

 **odd** **even**

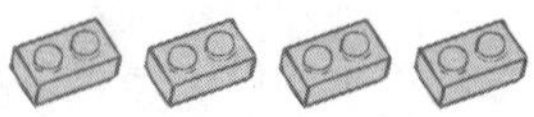 **odd** **even**

5. Circle the ways to make **7**.

5 + 2	4 + 4	6 + 1
9 – 2	3 + 5	7 + 0

1. Mark has to buy two new tires for his bike. If each tire costs $10.00, how much money does Mark need?

$__________

2. Mark has $15.00 in his bank, and he got $5.00 for doing jobs. Can he buy the tires?

○ **yes** ○ **no**

Explain:

____

____

____

____

WEEK 14 DAY 1 Daily Math Practice

1 3 + 9 = ____

9 + 3 = ____

2 15 + 1 = ____

____ − 1 = 15

3 Sammy found two nickels in his pocket. How much did he find?

____¢

4 Draw an **X** on the seventh bird.

5 5 10 15 ____ ____ ____

____ ____ ____ ____

____ ____ ____ ____

WEEK 14 DAY 2 Daily Math Practice

1 2 + 9 = ____

2 + 10 = ____

2 + 11 = ____

2

$$\begin{array}{r} 11 \\ -\ 5 \\ \hline \end{array} \qquad \begin{array}{r} 11 \\ -\ 6 \\ \hline \end{array}$$

3 Which is heavier?

10 pounds   100 pounds

4 Write the time.

9:00

____ o'clock

5 There were six flowers in the vase. Two of the flowers were roses. How many flowers were **not** roses?

____ flowers

1. 5 + 6 = ____

   6 + 5 = ____

2. 16 – 8 = ____

   8 + ____ = 16

3. Trina saw three pigs, two cows, and four chickens on the farm. How many animals did she see in all?

   ____ animals

4. Draw a rectangle.

   Write how many.

   ____ sides ____ corners

5. 12 = 4 + 8 ○ **yes** ○ **no**

   8 = 12 + 4 ○ **yes** ○ **no**

   12 = 8 + 4 ○ **yes** ○ **no**

1. 7 – 5 = ____

   8 – 5 = ____

2. 4 + 8 = ____

3. Five pairs of ants marched up the hill. How many ants were there in all?

   ____ ants

4. Circle the ways to make **nine**.

   3 + 6 4 + 5 2 + 7

   1 + 7 0 + 9 4 + 4

5. How much?

   ____ cents

1. How many toes?

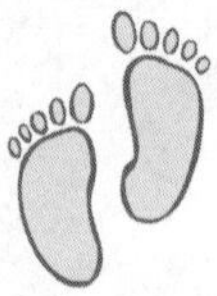

____ toes

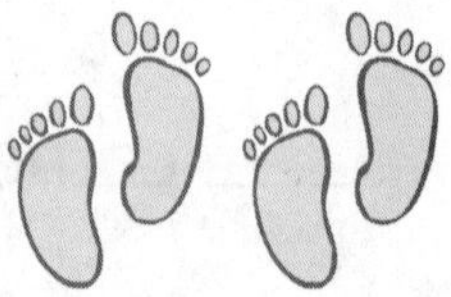

____ toes

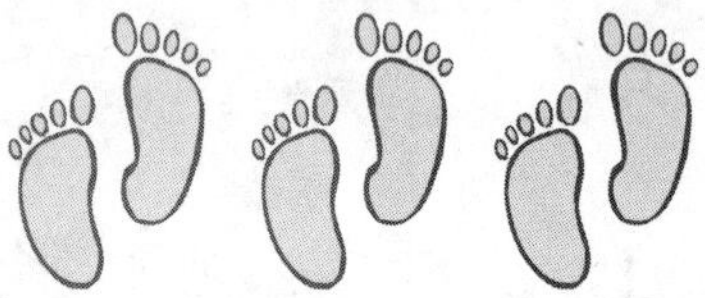

____ toes

How many toes do 5 babies have? ____ toes

2. How many ears?

____ ears

____ ears

____ ears

How many ears do 6 rabbits have? ____ ears

WEEK 15 DAY 1 Daily Math Practice

1. 5 + 7 = 11 + 0

   ○ yes ○ no

2. 10 – 3 = _____

   20 – 3 = _____

3. There were two goldfish and four red fish in the bowl. How many fish were there in all?

   _____ fish

4. Are the two sides the same?

○ yes ○ no

○ yes ○ no

5. Finish the pattern.

WEEK 15 DAY 2 Daily Math Practice

1. 5 + 8 = _____

   8 + 5 = _____

2. 4 – 4 = _____

   25 – 25 = _____

3. The bag had ten cookies in it. If Eli ate two and Molly ate one, how many cookies were left?

   _____ cookies

4. Mark the pizza divided in half.

○ 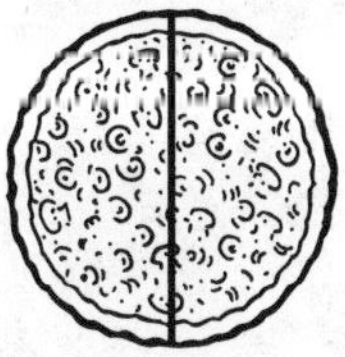 ○ 

5. Write the number.

   eleven _____

   thirteen _____

   fourteen _____

WEEK 15 DAY 3 Daily Math Practice

1 $7 + 5 =$ ____

____ $- 7 = 5$

2 $4 + 2 + 1 =$ ____

3 $9 < 3$ ○ **yes** ○ **no**

$19 > 13$ ○ **yes** ○ **no**

4 About how many paper clips?.

○ 5

○ 15

○ 50

5 Bingo hid four bones in the garden and two bones in the park. How many bones did he hide in all?

____ bones

WEEK 15 DAY 4 Daily Math Practice

1

$$\begin{array}{r} 4 \\ +\,9 \\ \hline \end{array} \qquad \begin{array}{r} 5 \\ +\,8 \\ \hline \end{array} \qquad \begin{array}{r} 6 \\ +\,7 \\ \hline \end{array}$$

2 $18 - 1 = 17 + 0$

○ **yes** ○ **no**

3 Four trucks and six cars were stopped at a light. How many vehicles were stopped in all?

____ vehicles

4 Write four number sentences using **3**, **5**, and **8**.

____ + ____ = ____

____ + ____ = ____

____ − ____ = ____

____ − ____ = ____

5 Are both sides the same?

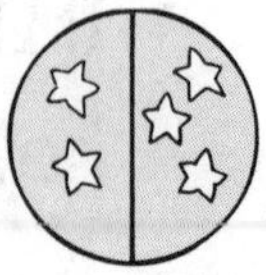

○ **yes** ○ **no**

➤ Activity 1

 = 1 birthday

March						
Sun.	Mon.	Tues.	Wed.	Thurs.	Fri.	Sat.
			1	2	3	 4
5	6	 7	8	9	10	11
12	13	 14	15	16	 17	18
19	20	21	22	23	24	25
26	27	 28	29	30	31	

1. How many birthdays are there in March? _____ birthdays

2. What day of the week has the most birthdays?

   ○ Sunday ○ Tuesday ○ Friday

3. There is only one birthday on the weekend. ○ **yes** ○ **no**

➤ Activity 2

Use this number line to mark **yes** or **no** for each number sentence.

1. $10 > 11$ ○ **yes** ○ **no**
2. $14 = 13 + 1$ ○ **yes** ○ **no**
3. $12 < 9$ ○ **yes** ○ **no**
4. $7 > 3$ ○ **yes** ○ **no**

1 6 + 8 = _____

8 + 6 = _____

2 15 − 7 = _____

_____ + 7 = 15

3 What comes next?

2 4 6 8 10 12 14 _____

4 Which shows $\frac{1}{4}$?

○ 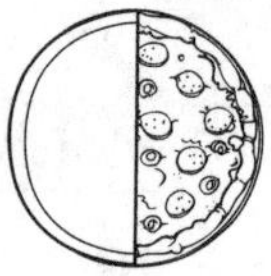

○ 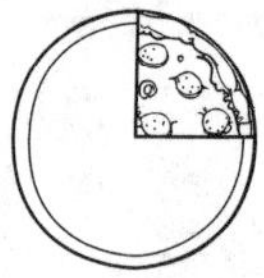

5 Keli is 11. Her sister is 6. How many years older than her sister is Keli?

_____ years older

1 7 + 7 = _____

7 − 7 = _____

2 10 + 10 + 10 = _____

3 Tony swam four laps of freestyle and six laps of backstroke. How many laps did he swim in all?

_____ laps

4 Continue the pattern.

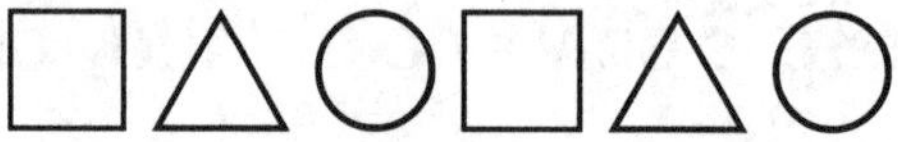

_____ _____ _____

5 How many?

○ 11 ○ 12 ○ 21

1 7 – 6 = 1 + 0

○ **yes** ○ **no**

2 9 + 3 = _____

9 + 4 = _____

3 I have seven sharp pencils and two broken pencils. How many pencils do I have in all?

_____ pencils

4 If 53 + 4 = 57, then 57 – 4 = _____.

5 Write the number.

four _____

twenty-one _____

thirty _____

thirty-two _____

1 6 + 10 = _____

6 + 9 = _____

2 10 – 2 = 7 – 0

○ **yes** ○ **no**

3 Jamal hit three balls. Ann hit four balls. Terri didn't get a hit. How many hits were there in all?

_____ hits

4 What time is it?

_____ o'clock

5 Color the bigger square.

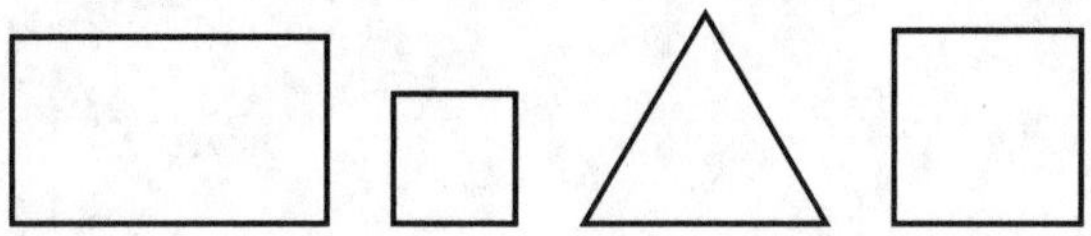

On Monday, four girls checked out 3 books each.
On Tuesday, two of the girls returned their books.

1. How many books are still checked out? _____ books

Show your work here.

2. Each girl reads 3 books every day. How many books will each girl read in 3 days?

_____ books

1 7 + 8 = ____ ____ − 7 = 8

2 9 + 2 = 11 + 0

○ **yes** ○ **no**

3 Two polar bears were walking across the ice. Six more polar bears joined them. How many were there in all?

____ polar bears

4 35 34 33 ____ ____ ____

____ ____ ____

5 Write four number sentences using **6**, **5**, and **11**.

____ + ____ = ____

____ + ____ = ____

____ − ____ = ____

____ − ____ = ____

1 15 − 7 = ____ 15 − 8 = ____

2 9 + 5 = ____

7 + 7 = ____

3 Each drummer needs two drumsticks. How many drumsticks do five drummers need?

____ drumsticks

4 3 + 3 + 3 = ____

4 + 4 + 4 = ____

5 Write an addition story to tell about the fish.

____

____

____

1. 9 + 7 = _____

2. 9 – 2 = _____

   2 + _____ = 9

3. Juanita had three cupcakes. She gave one to Felix and two to the twins. How many cupcakes did she have left?

   _____ cupcakes

4. 10 20 30 _____ _____ _____

   _____ _____ _____ _____

5. How many sides?

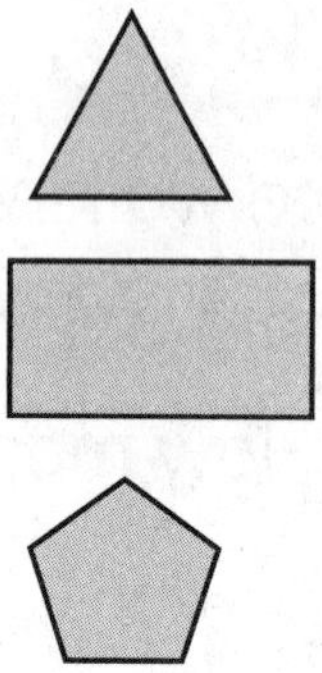

_____

_____

_____

1. 8 + 5 = _____

2. 20 – 10 = _____

3. The hungry caterpillar ate three leaves, two strawberries, and five grapes. How many things did it eat in all?

   _____ things

4. Write the rule for each group.

Group 1

____

____

____

Group 2

____

____

____

5. If 34 + 7 = 41, then

   41 – _____ = 34.

1. Measure the **longest** side of a book with your pencil.

My book is _____ pencils long.

2. Look at the picture to answer the questions.

a.

b.

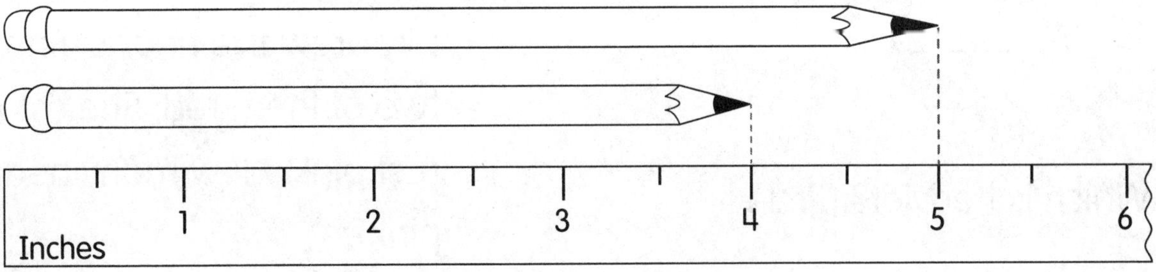

Color the longer pencil yellow.

Color the shorter pencil red.

How long is each pencil? **a.** _____ inches **b.** _____ inches

How much longer is the yellow pencil than the red pencil?

_____ inch longer

3. Add or subtract.

2 inches	5 inches	3 inches
+ 3 inches	− 1 inch	+ 3 inches
☐ inches	☐ inches	☐ inches

1. $7 + 9 =$ ____

   $7 + 11 =$ ____

2. $15 - 9 =$ ____

   $15 - 6 =$ ____

3. Which is heavier? Circle it.

2 grams	51 pounds
20 grams	15 pounds

4. Draw an **X** on the eighth bead.

first →
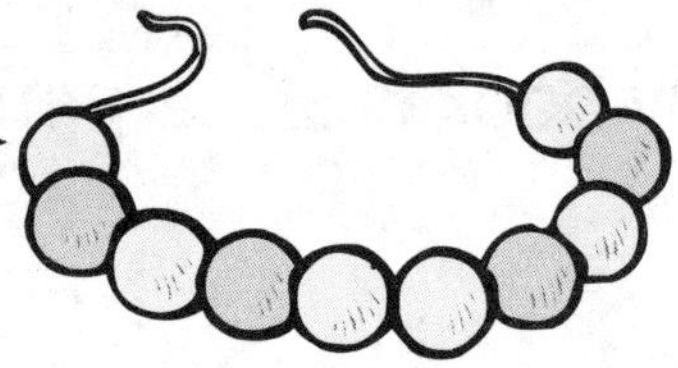

5. Lilly drew five hearts. She colored two of them red. She colored the rest pink. How many hearts are pink?

____ pink hearts

1. $\begin{array}{r} 10 \\ +\ 0 \\ \hline \end{array}$ $\quad \begin{array}{r} 10 \\ +\ 5 \\ \hline \end{array}$ $\quad \begin{array}{r} 10 \\ +10 \\ \hline \end{array}$

2. If $17 - 5 = 12$, then $12 + 5 =$ ____.

3. Circle the one that does **not** belong.

4. What time is it?

____ o'clock

5. Mike invited seven friends to his party. Two cannot come. How many friends will be there?

____ friends

1. 9 + 8 = ____

   ____ − 9 = 8

2. 5 + 10 = ____

   ____ − 5 = 10

3. Count by 5s.

   50 55 ____ ____ ____

   ____ ____

4. ____ tens + ____ ones = 76

   ____ tens + ____ ones = 50

5. David bought two apples for $1.00. How much would four apples cost?

   $________

1. 5 + 10 = ____

   5 + 9 = ____

2. 8 − 7 = ____

   15 − 14 = ____

3. Circle the ways to make **eleven**.

10 + 1	12 − 2	5 + 6
11 + 0	15 − 4	9 + 1

4. A square has ____ sides.

   A triangle has ____ sides.

5. Four bees flew to three flowers. How many more bees are there than flowers?

   ____ more bee

1. How many squares in all? _____ squares

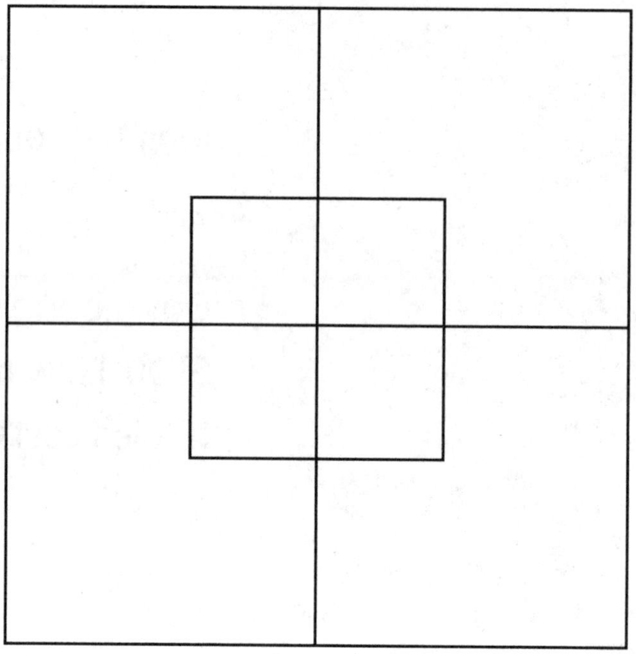

2. How many squares in all? _____ squares

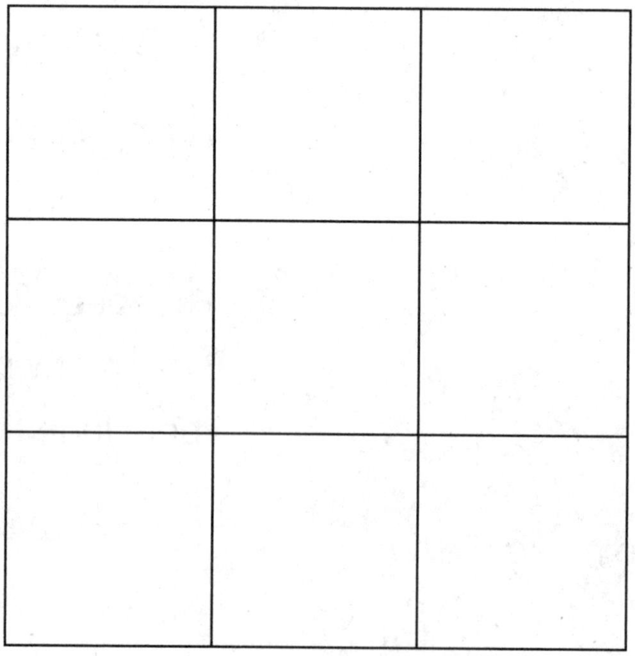

1. $8 + 8 =$ ____

   $9 + 9 =$ ____

2. $6 - 3 =$ ____

   $8 - 4 =$ ____

3. Six girls formed two equal teams. How many girls were on each team?

   ____ girls

4. If $36 + 42 = 78$, then

   $42 +$ ____ $= 78$.

5. Color $\frac{1}{2}$ of the rectangle.

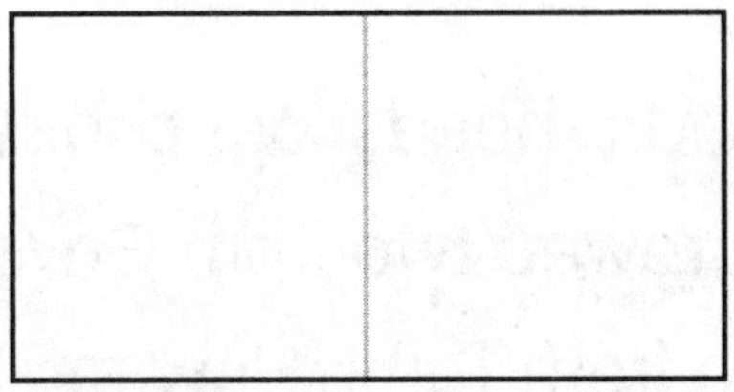

$\frac{1}{2} < 1$ whole

○ **yes** ○ **no**

1. $5 + 5 =$ ____

   $6 + 5 =$

2. $12 - 2 =$ ____

3. Carrie planted three rows of tulips. She put six bulbs in each row. How many bulbs did she plant in all?

   ____ bulbs

4. Write a subtraction story for the picture.

____

____

____

____

5. What is 10 more than 20? ____

WEEK 19 DAY 3 Daily Math Practice

1. 13 – 9 = _____

2. How many in all?

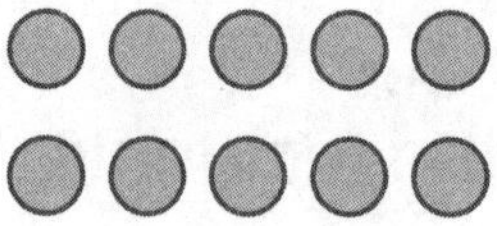 = _____

3. Kendra needs four chairs. She borrowed two from Gavin and two from Tami. How many more chairs does she need?

_____ more chairs

4. 14 = 15 ○ yes ○ no

$14 < 15$ ○ yes ○ no

$14 > 15$ ○ yes ○ no

5. About how many pounds of potatoes?

1 pound

10 pounds

100 pounds

WEEK 19 DAY 4 Daily Math Practice

1. 8 – 1 = 10 – 1

○ yes ○ no

2. 10 – 5 = _____

20 – 5 = _____

3. Color the squares red.
Color the rectangles yellow.

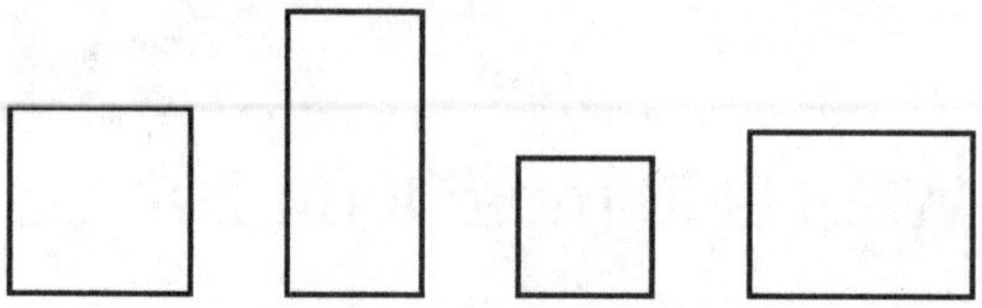

4. Are both sides the same?

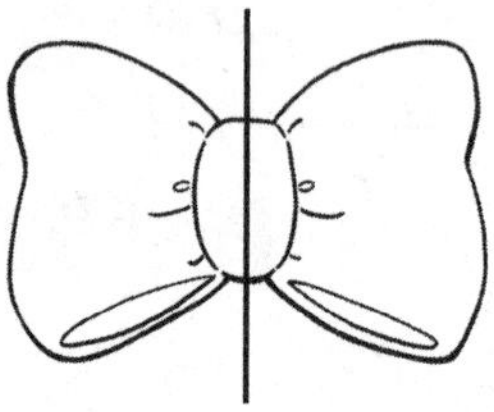

○ yes ○ no

5. Brad checked out five books and James checked out three books. How many books did they check out altogether?

_____ books

Look at the graph to answer the questions.

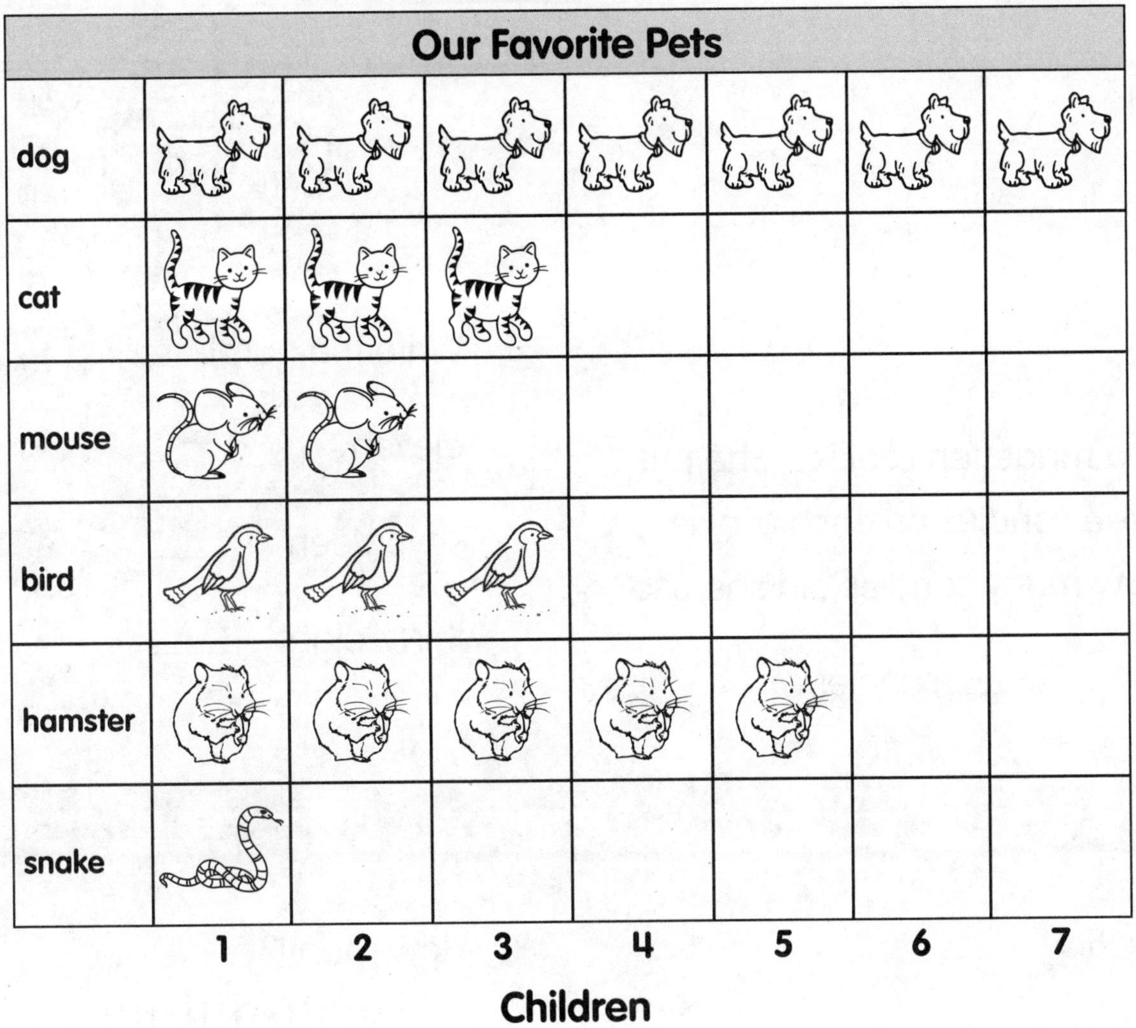

1. Which pet is the most favorite? ____________

2. Which pet is the least favorite? ____________

3. Which **two** pets were picked by the same number of children?

____________ and ____________

4. Write something else you learned from the graph.

____

____

1 13 – 2 = ____

2 + ____ = 13

2 6 + 10 = ____

7 + 10 = ____

3 Bea made ten cookies. She put three candies on each cookie. How many candies did she use?

____ candies

4 Color $\frac{1}{4}$.

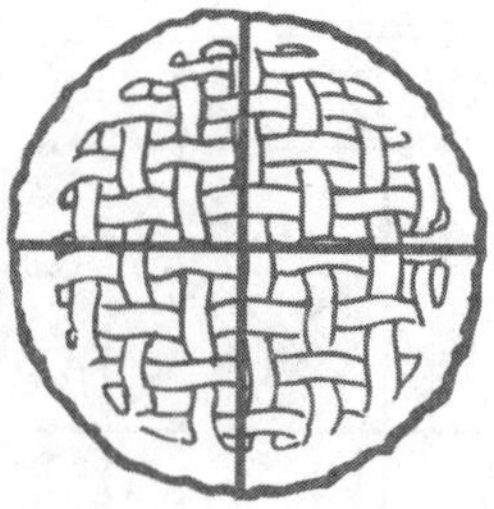

5 Write the numbers.

eleven ____

seventeen ____

thirty-eight ____

1 4 + 8 = ____

____ – 8 = 4

2 15 – 4 = ____

3 Continue the pattern.

____ ____ ____

4 How many?

____ tally marks

5 The bus had fifteen passengers. Four got off at the first stop. Two got off at the second stop. How many passengers were left?

____ passengers

WEEK 20 DAY 3 — Daily Math Practice

1 2 + 9 = 11 + 0

○ yes ○ no

2

$$\begin{array}{r} 8 \\ -\ 6 \\ \hline \end{array} \qquad \begin{array}{r} 18 \\ -\ 6 \\ \hline \end{array}$$

3 Bob piled blocks in stacks of five. He made six stacks. How many blocks did he use in all?

_____ blocks

4 2 _____ 6 _____ 10 _____ 14

_____ 18 _____

5 Color the cones.

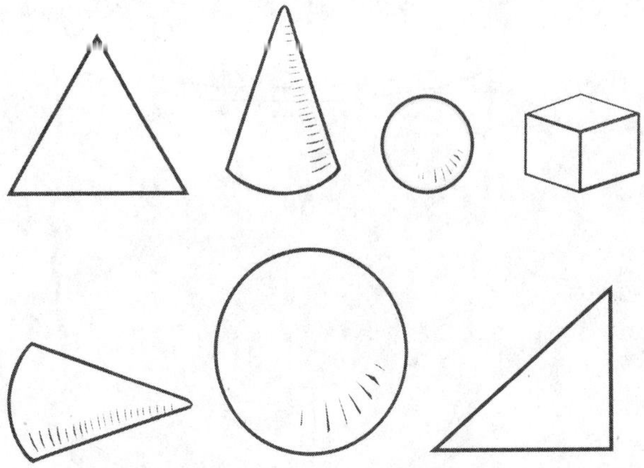

WEEK 20 DAY 4 — Daily Math Practice

1 100 + 4 = _____

2

$$\begin{array}{r} 5 \\ 1 \\ +\ 2 \\ \hline \end{array} \qquad \begin{array}{r} 5 \\ +\ 3 \\ \hline \end{array}$$

3 Ten balls were in the box. The first graders are using seven of them. How many balls are left?

_____ balls

4 Write the time.

_____ o'clock

5 If 20 + 30 = 50,

then 50 – _____ = 20.

1. Doug went fishing. He had 12 worms in a can and 3 in his pocket.

Draw Doug's worms.

2. Doug put a new worm on the hook after every fish he got. He has four worms left. How many fish did he get?

_____ fish

Show your work here.

WEEK 21 DAY 1 Daily Math Practice

1 7 + 10 = _____

17 + 10 = _____

2 6 – 5 = 16 – 15

○ yes

○ no

3 Rick has two bags of cans to recycle. Joe has three bags. How many bags do they have in all?

_____ bags

4 Draw an **X** on the closed figures.

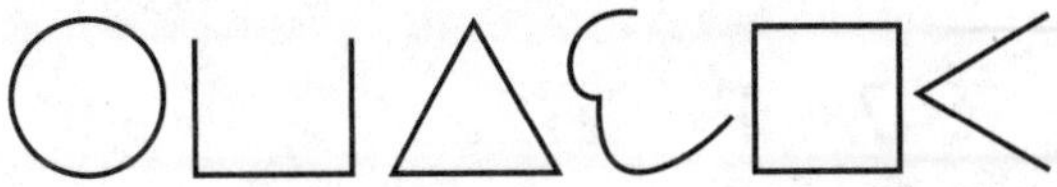

5 Write four number sentences using **6**, **2**, and **8**.

_____ + _____ = _____

_____ + _____ = _____

_____ – _____ = _____

_____ – _____ = _____

WEEK 21 DAY 2 Daily Math Practice

1 6 + 7 = _____

7 + 6 = _____

2 3 + 8 + 2 = _____

3 1 ten = _____ 4 tens = _____

2 tens = _____ 5 tens = _____

3 tens = _____ 6 tens = _____

4 Mark the pattern unit.

○ AB ○ ABB ○ AABB

5 Bill walked four blocks to Sam's house, and then he walked back home. How many blocks did he walk in all?

_____ blocks

1. 647 + 0 = ______

   647 + 1 = ______

2. 8 + 6 = ______

   18 + 6 = ______

3. Which stem is longer?

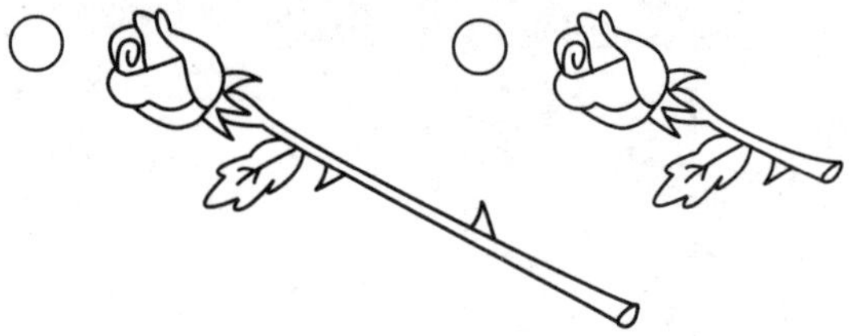

4. If 7 + 3 = 10, then

   ______ – ______ = 7.

5. Tom put three balls, one jump rope, and four beanbags into the bin. How many toys did Tom put into the bin in all?

   ______ toys

1. 8 + 9 = ______

2. 10 – 6 = ______

3. How much?

   ______ cents

4. **Five** is an odd number.

   ○ **yes** ○ **no**

5. Terri and her sister have two bikes and a wagon. How many wheels are there altogether?

   ______ wheels

1. The cook needs one cup of cheese for each pizza. Each package of cheese holds four cups. The class ordered eight pizzas. How many packages of cheese will the cook need?

____ packages

Show your work here.

2. Mark the pizza that shows fourths.

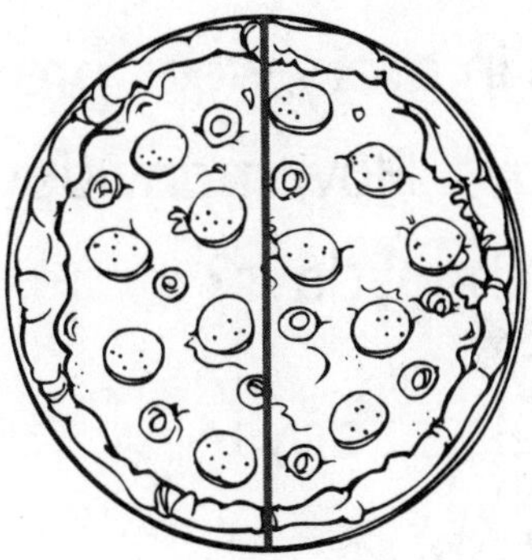

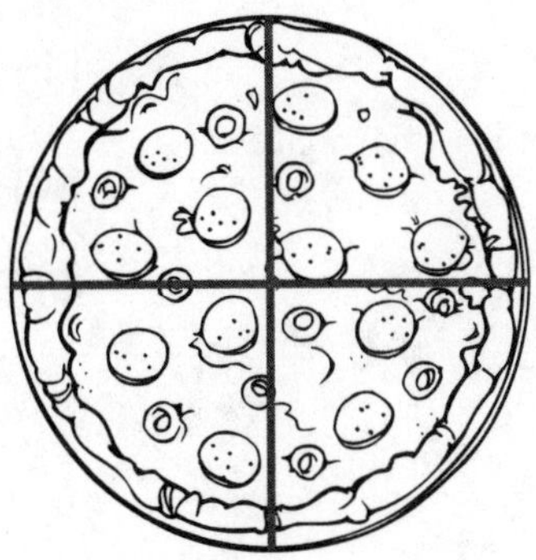

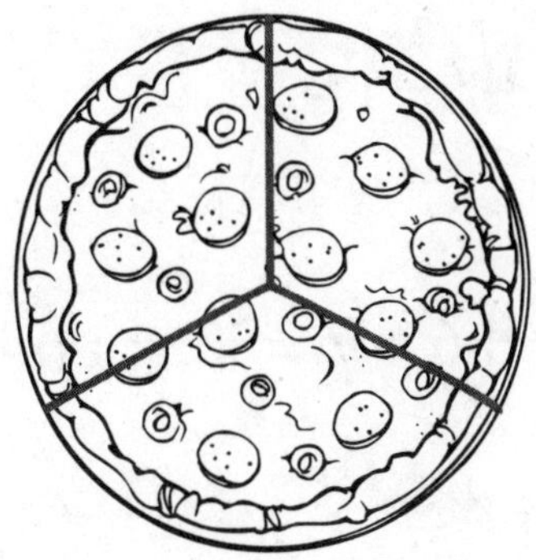

1 $50 + 10 =$ _____

2 $10 + 1 =$ _____

$10 + 2 =$ _____

$10 + 3 =$ _____

3 Draw an **X** on the heaviest.

4 Write the time.

_____ o'clock

5 The ball box has two basketballs, three tennis balls, five soccer balls, and one baseball. How many balls are there in all?

_____ balls

1 $9 + 3 =$ _____

_____ $- 9 = 3$

2 $23 - 1 =$ _____

$47 - 1 =$ _____

3 If $6 + 7 = 13$, then $13 -$ _____ $= 6$.

4 Write 5 more.

20 _____ 40 _____

30 _____ 50 _____

5 Five days in every week are school days. How many days are **not** school days?

_____ days

1 1 ten + 6 ones = _____

2 17 – 7 = _____

7 + _____ = 17

3 Chuck planted four trees. One tree died, so he planted another one. How many trees did he plant in all?

_____ trees

4 How much?

_____ cents

5 Circle the ways to make **8**.

5 + 3	2 + 7	4 + 4
6 + 1	8 + 0	16 – 7

1 4 + 7 + 3 = _____

2 10 – 0 = _____ 10 – 3 = _____

10 – 1 = _____ 10 – 4 = _____

10 – 2 = _____ 10 – 5 = _____

3 The fourth mitten has stripes.

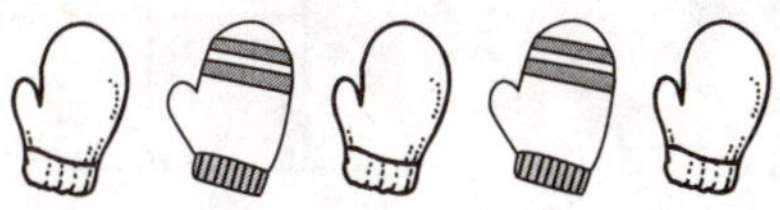

○ **yes** ○ **no**

4 Circle the straight lines.

5 Cam and Jack took five boxes to the recycling center. The man paid them $1.00. If they share the money equally, how much will each boy get?

_____¢

➤ Activity 1

1. Mark the name of the solid figure.

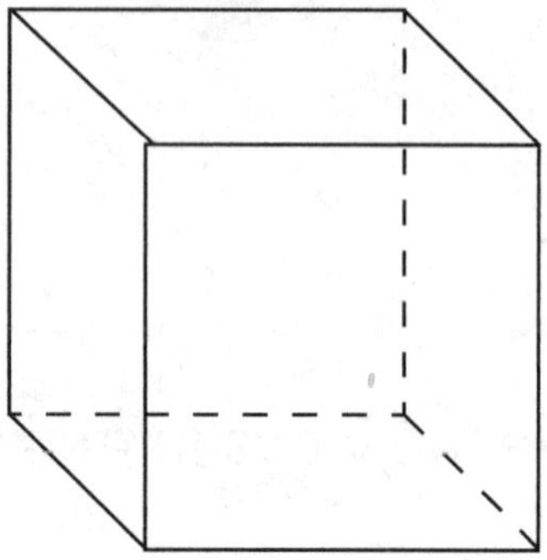

○ cube

○ sphere

○ square

2. How many sides? _____

3. Can it stack? ○ **yes** ○ **no**

4. Can it roll? ○ **yes** ○ **no**

➤ Activity 2

Tess built this stack of cubes.

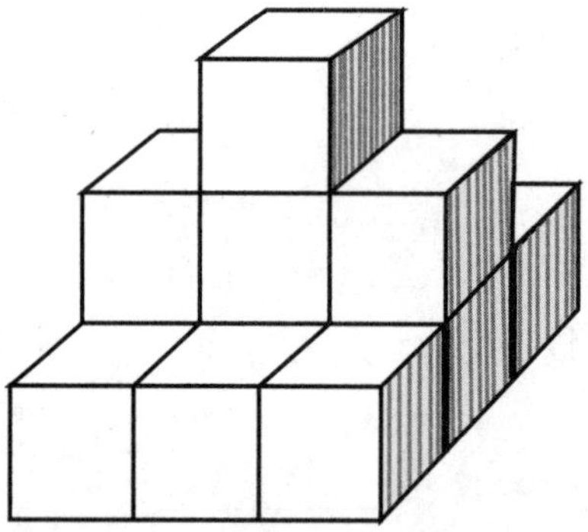

Which drawing shows how the stack looks from the shaded side?

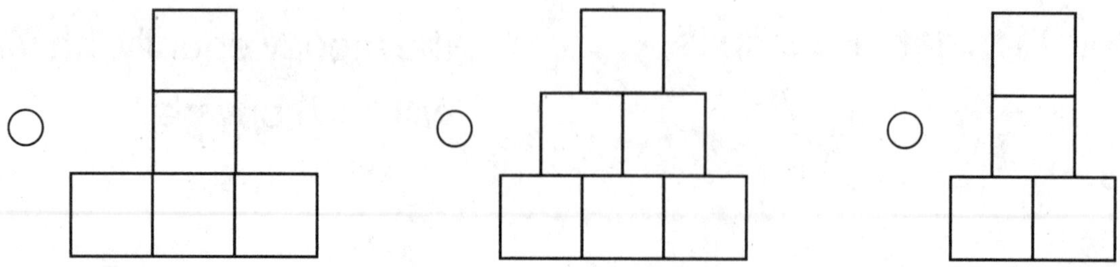

1. 10 + 8 = _____

   12 + 8 = _____

2. 8 – 0 = _____

   18 – 8 = _____

3. Three birds each laid three eggs. How many eggs are there in all?

   _____ eggs

4. Color $\frac{1}{2}$ of all the pigs.

5. Write the number.

   zero _____

   eight _____

   twenty-four _____

   forty-two _____

1. $\begin{array}{r} 6 \\ +\,7 \\ \hline \end{array}$ $\qquad$ $\begin{array}{r} 7 \\ +\,6 \\ \hline \end{array}$

2. 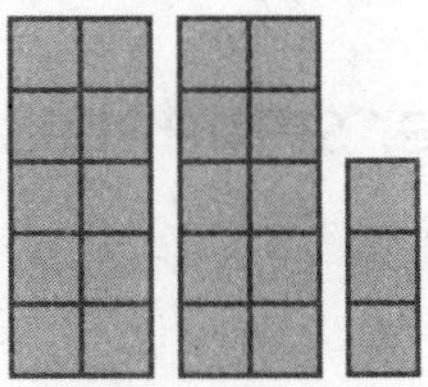

   _____ tens + _____ ones = _____

3. Are both sides the same?

   ○ **yes** ○ **no**

4. Circle the time.

   6:30

   7:30

   8:30

5. Pam gives her dog a bone every morning and every night. How many bones does she give her dog in one week?

   _____ bones

WEEK 23 DAY 3 Daily Math Practice

1 $9 + 7 =$ ____

2 How many in all?

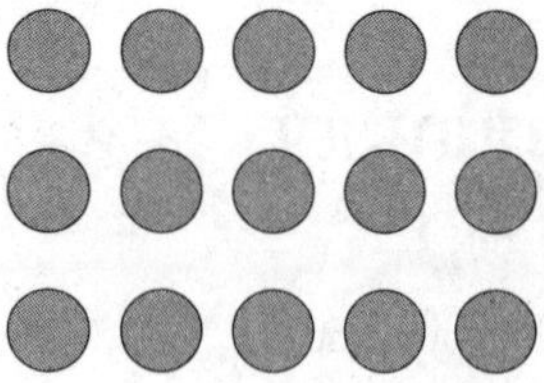 = ____

3 Continue the pattern.

 ____ ____

4 Color the rectangles.

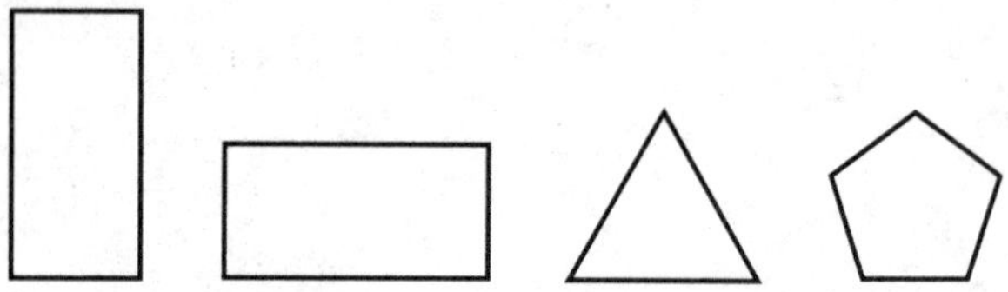

5 The nurse saw 4 boys and 6 girls with colds. How many children did she see in all?

____ children

WEEK 23 DAY 4 Daily Math Practice

1 $15 - 6 =$ ____

$6 +$ ____ $= 15$

2 $2 + 7 + 4 =$ ____

3 Angela has four pink jelly beans and five purple jelly beans. If she eats three jelly beans, how many will she have left?

____ jelly beans

4 $9 + 10 =$ ____

$10 + 10 =$ ____

5 Write four number sentences using **2**, **7**, and **9**.

____ + ____ = ____

____ + ____ = ____

____ − ____ = ____

____ − ____ = ____

Circle **yes** if both sides are the same.

Circle **no** if both sides are **not** the same.

1.

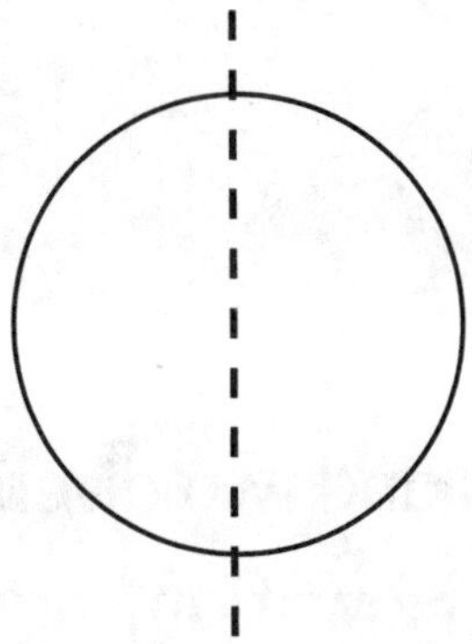

○ **yes** ○ **no**

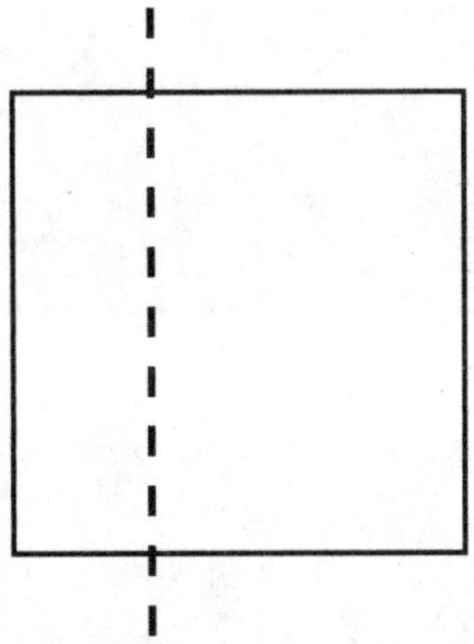

○ **yes** ○ **no**

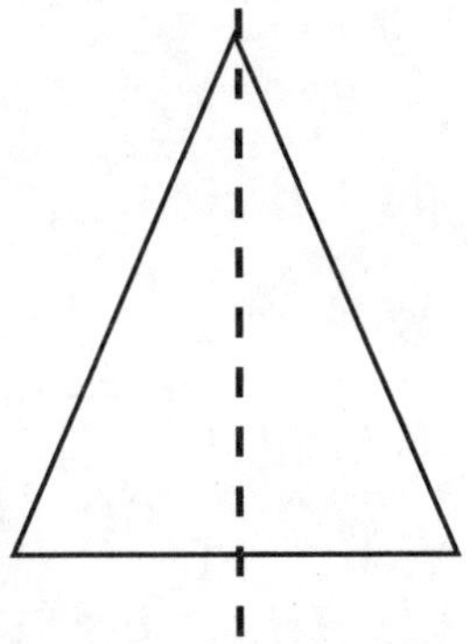

○ **yes** ○ **no**

2.

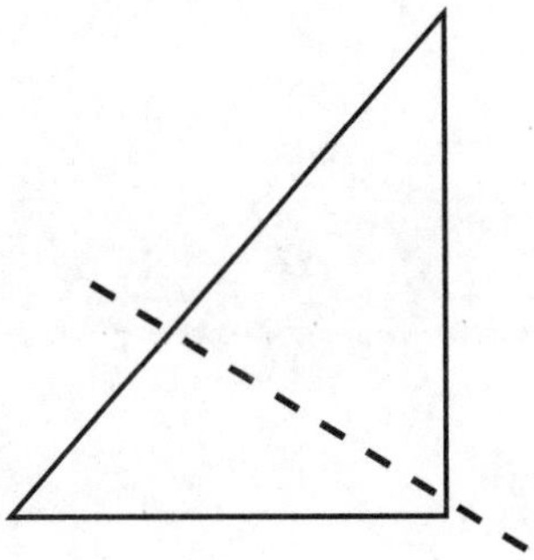

○ **yes** ○ **no**

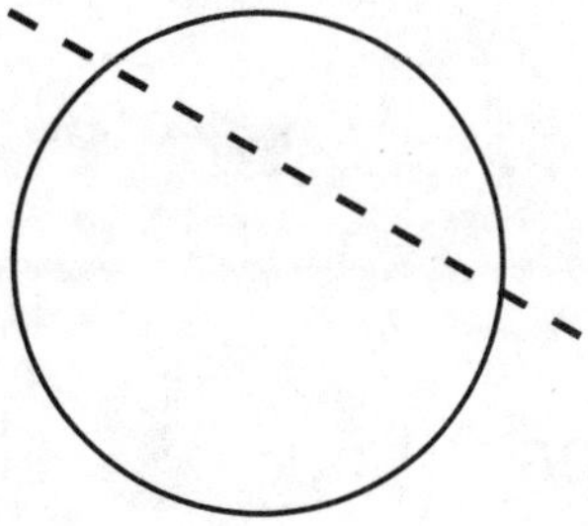

○ **yes** ○ **no**

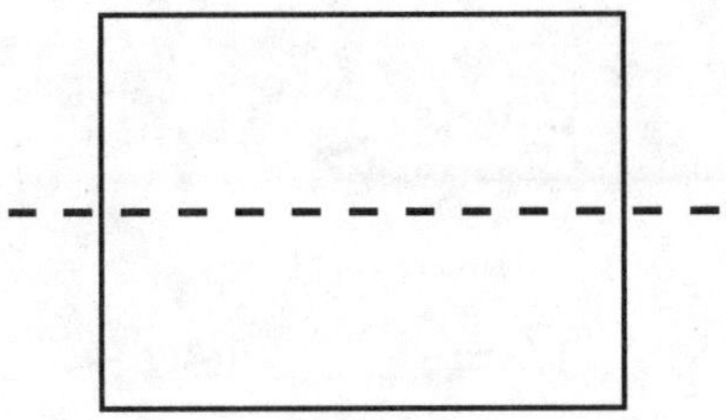

○ **yes** ○ **no**

3.

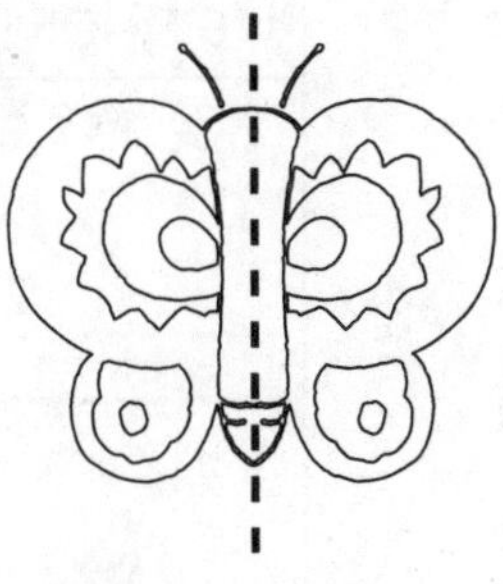

○ **yes** ○ **no**

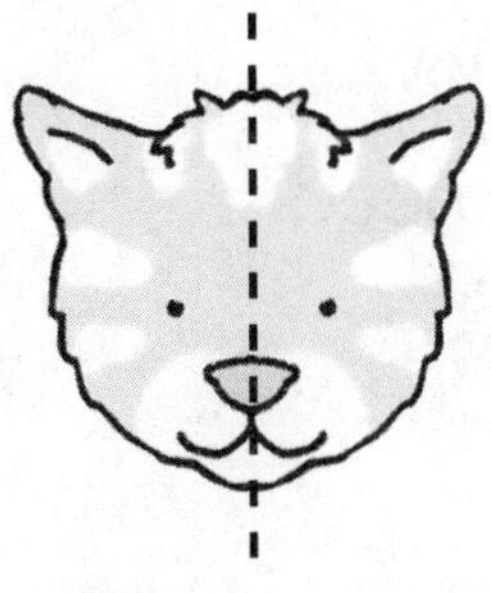

○ **yes** ○ **no**

○ **yes** ○ **no**

WEEK 24 DAY 1 Daily Math Practice

1. $7 + 4 =$ _____

   _____ $- 7 = 4$

2. $14 - 8 =$ _____

   $14 - 10 =$ _____

3. $34 > 31$ ○ **yes** ○ **no**

   $27 > 72$ ○ **yes** ○ **no**

4. Color $\frac{1}{4}$ of all the balls.

5. One octopus and two divers are in the water. How many arms are there in all?

   _____ arms

WEEK 24 DAY 2 Daily Math Practice

1. $17 =$ _____ ten + _____ ones

2. $18 - 9 =$ _____

3. The truck holds ten crates, and the driver has loaded six. How many more crates does he need for a full load?

   _____ crates

4. How many?

   _____ tally marks

5.

ten more
6 _____
30 _____

ten less
_____ 39
_____ 97

1. $9 + 8 = 10 + 7$ ○ **yes** ○ **no**

2. $8 - 3 =$ _____

   _____ $+ 3 = 8$

3. Todd has three pencils, four markers, and twenty-two crayons. How many drawing tools does he have?

   _____ drawing tools

4. Circle the time.

1:00

1:30

6:00

5. If $23 + 5 = 28$,

   then $28 -$ _____ $= 23$.

1. $7 + 7 =$ _____

   $8 + 8 =$

2. $18 - 5 =$ _____

3. Two frogs ate six flies. If each frog ate the same number of flies, how many did each frog eat?

   _____ flies

4. $69 < 50$ ○ **yes** ○ **no**

   $47 < 74$ ○ **yes** ○ **no**

5. Continue the pattern.

△ ○ ○ □ △ ○ ○ □

_____ _____ _____ _____

Each group of students planted ten seeds. Each seed can make one sprout. How many sprouting seeds did each group have?

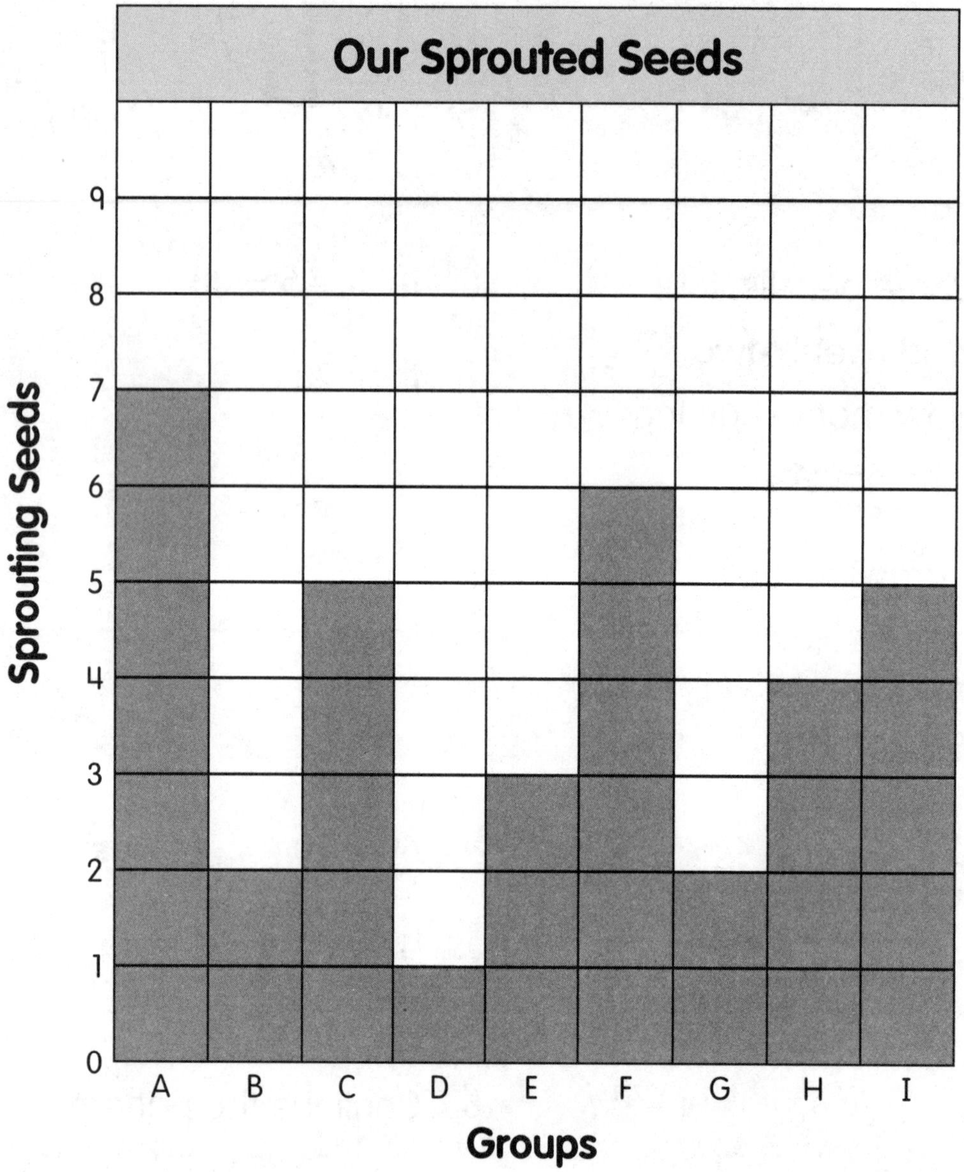

Group A ____ Group B ____ Group C ____

Group D ____ Group E ____ Group F ____

Group G ____ Group H ____ Group I ____

1

$$\begin{array}{r} 9 \\ -\ 5 \\ \hline \end{array} \qquad \begin{array}{r} 19 \\ -\ 5 \\ \hline \end{array}$$

2 Luke has two boards. He needs four nails for each board. How many nails does he need?

_____ nails

3

$$\begin{array}{r} 6 \\ +\ 5 \\ \hline \end{array} \qquad \begin{array}{r} 8 \\ +\ 7 \\ \hline \end{array} \qquad \begin{array}{r} 9 \\ +\ 8 \\ \hline \end{array}$$

4 How much?

_____ cents

5 65 64 63 _____ _____ _____

_____ _____ _____ _____ _____

1 2 + 4 – 2 + 1 = _____

2 Mark the pattern unit.

○ AAB ○ AABC ○ ABC

3 If 5 + 23 = 28,

then 23 + 5 = _____.

4 Color the half circles.

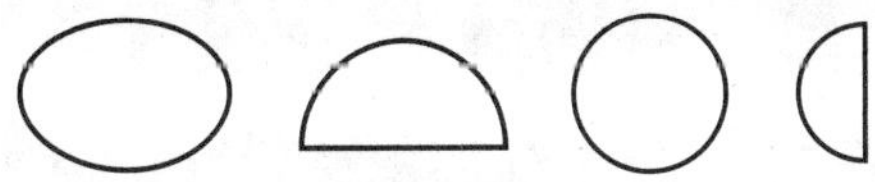

5 There are six books on the table, three books on the chair, and ten books on the shelf. How many books are there in all?

_____ books

WEEK 25 DAY 3 Daily Math Practice

1 $3 + 7 =$ ____

2 $8{,}247 + 0 =$ ______

3 Show four ways to make **12**.

____ + ____ = 12

____ + ____ = 12

____ − ____ = 12

____ − ____ = 12

4 Draw an **X** on the line that is 2 paper clips long.

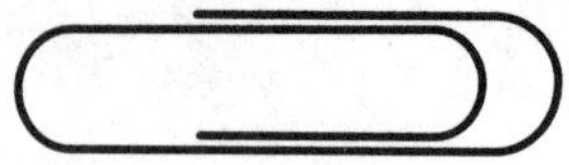

A ________

B ____________________________

C _______________

5 **6** is an odd number.

○ **yes** ○ **no**

WEEK 25 DAY 4 Daily Math Practice

1 $17 - 9 =$ ____

2

$$\begin{array}{r} 7 \\ 6 \\ +\ 4 \\ \hline \end{array} \qquad \begin{array}{r} 7 \\ +\ 10 \\ \hline \end{array}$$

3 Scott put six books, three pencils, and a notebook in his backpack. How many school supplies are in his backpack?

____ school supplies

4 $100 + 10 + 9 = ?$

○ 100 ○ 119 ○ 19

5 How long is the gum?

____ centimeters

➤ Activity 1

What does **not** belong? Draw an **X** on it.

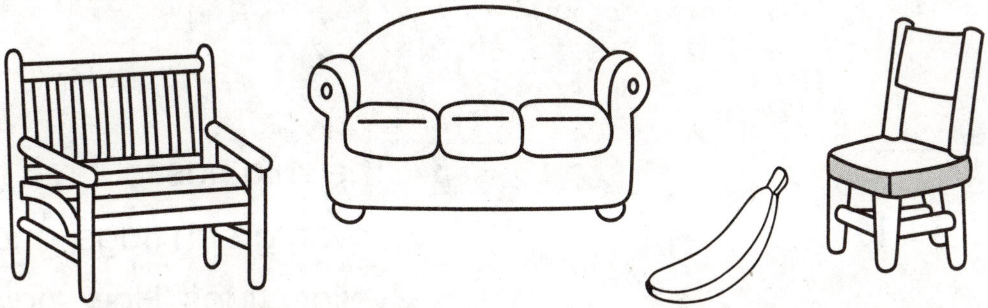

Tell how the other things are alike.

____

____

➤ Activity 2

The dog ate my 100s chart!

Write the missing numbers.

		49	50
	58		
67			70
	78		

1. 9 + 10 = ____

   10 + 10 = ____

2. 16 – 8 = ____

   8 + ____ = 16

3. 20 ____ ____ 35

   ____ 45 ____

4. Circle the second star.

5. The ship has four red flags, seven green flags, and three yellow flags. How many flags does the ship have in all?

   ____ flags

1. 8 + 5 = ____

2. 9 + 6 = ____

3. Write **<** or **>** to tell the rule:

   Group A
   1, 4, 3, 6, 2, 5

   All numbers are ____ 7.

   Group B
   8, 10, 9, 11, 13, 12

   All numbers are ____ 7.

4. Draw an **X** on the heaviest.

5. Each lunch bag has two sandwiches in it. How many sandwiches are in six bags?

   ____ sandwiches

WEEK 26 DAY 3 Daily Math Practice

1. 13 – 4 = ____

   13 – 3 = ____

2. If 41 + 8 = ____, then

   ____ – 8 = 41.

3. The ladder has 18 rungs. Tom climbed halfway up. How many rungs did he climb?

   ____ rungs

4. 2 + 20 = ____   4 + 20 = ____

   3 + 20 = ____   5 + 20 = ____

5. Color the circle green.
   Color the triangle black.
   Color the square pink.

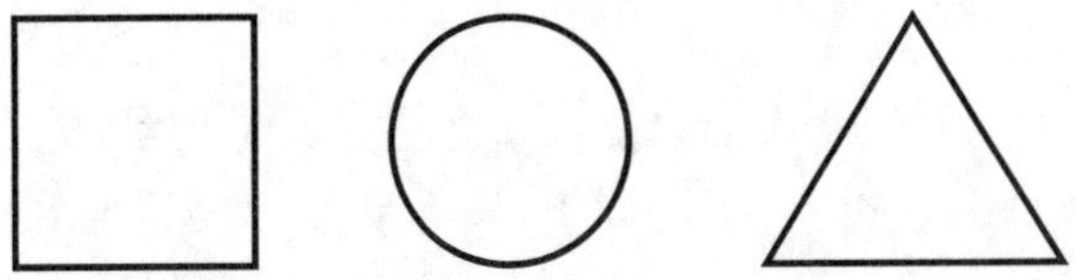

WEEK 26 DAY 4 Daily Math Practice

1. 17 – 8 = ____

   8 + ____ = 17

2. 10 + 9 = ____

3. Mark the name for the shaded part.

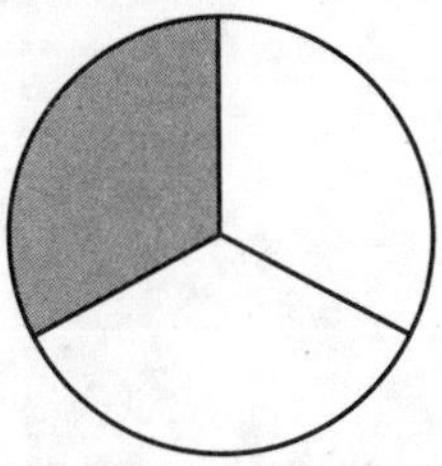

   ○ $\frac{1}{4}$

   ○ $\frac{1}{3}$

   ○ $\frac{1}{2}$

4. Five boys and seven girls sat in a row. Write a number sentence about the row.

   ____ + ____ = ____

5. Circle the ways to make **9**.

   8 + 1   7 – 2   3 + 6

   5 + 4   9 – 0   12 – 3

1. The soccer team scored four goals in their first game, five goals in their second game, and two goals in their third game. How many goals did they score in all?

_____ goals

Show your work here.

2. The team lost the third game. At least how many goals did the other team score?

_____ goals

Show your work here.

1. 18 + 4 = _____

   _____ − 18 = 4

2. 6 + 8 = _____

   _____ − 6 = 8

3. Troy has 3 yellow cars, 7 green cars, and 6 white cars. How many cars does he have in all?

   _____ cars

4. 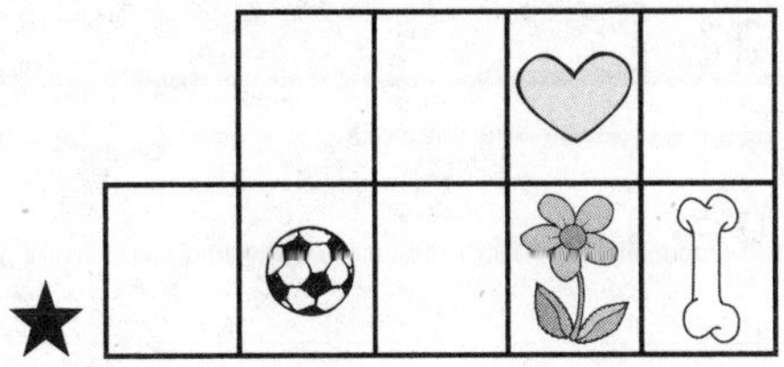

   Start at the star. Which answer tells how to find the ball?

   ○ left 2 boxes ○ right 2 boxes

5. Write the number.

   fifteen _____ sixty _____

   fifty _____

1. 7 + 3 = _____

   17 + 3 =

2. 12 − 7 = _____

   7 + _____ = 12

3. Harry caught two ants, three crickets, and six beetles. How many bugs did he catch in all?

   _____ bugs

4. $8 < 18$ ○ **yes** ○ **no**

   $24 > 42$ ○ **yes** ○ **no**

5. About how many cans of apple juice?

   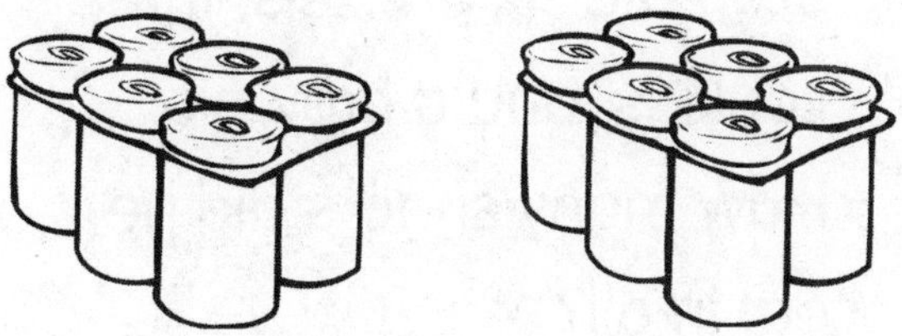

   6 12 18

WEEK 27 DAY 3 Daily Math Practice

1. 6 + 9 = ____

   9 + 6 = ____

2. 20 – 10 = ____

   30 – 10 = ____

3. Tim took four cookies. If he ate half of them, how many cookies did he eat?

   ____ cookies

4. Write a story problem for **6 – 2 = ?**

   ____

   ____

   ____

   ____

5. 5 + 4 = ____ + ____

   23 + 21 = ____ + ____

WEEK 27 DAY 4 Daily Math Practice

1. 7 + 8 = 10 + 5

   ○ **yes** ○ **no**

2. 17 – 8 = ____

3. Scott ate six pretzels, three cookies, and a brownie. How many snacks did he eat in all?

   ____ snacks

4. Write four number sentences using **6**, **9**, and **15**.

   ____ + ____ = ____

   ____ + ____ = ____

   ____ – ____ = ____

   ____ – ____ = ____

5. Are both sides the same?

   ○ **yes** ○ **no**

➤ Activity 1

Match the pattern to its name.

• ABC

• AB

• AAB

➤ Activity 2

Show ways to make **15**. Use **+** and **–**.

____ ◯ ____ = 15 ____ ◯ ____ = 15

____ ◯ ____ = 15 ____ ◯ ____ = 15

____ ◯ ____ = 15 ____ ◯ ____ = 15

____ ◯ ____ = 15 ____ ◯ ____ = 15

____ ◯ ____ = 15 ____ ◯ ____ = 15

1

$$\begin{array}{r} 13 \\ -\ 5 \\ \hline \end{array} \qquad \begin{array}{r} 15 \\ -\ 5 \\ \hline \end{array}$$

2 Count by 2s.

20 22 24 ____ ____

____ ____ ____ ____

3

$$\begin{array}{r} 12 \\ +\ 2 \\ \hline \end{array}$$

The sum is an even number.

○ **yes** ○ **no**

4 Write the number.

ninety-one ____

sixty-four ____

5 John ate $\frac{1}{2}$ of his sandwich for lunch and $\frac{1}{2}$ of his sandwich for a snack after school. How much is left?

________ is left

1 6 + 3 + 2 = ____

2 30 + 40 = ____

35 + 40 = ____

3 What comes next?

○ △ △ ○ △ △ ○ ____

 ____

4 How many?

____ tally marks

5 Juan had 105 marbles. His friend gave him 10 more. How many marbles does Juan have now?

______ marbles

1. 4 + 7 = ____

   11 − 7 = ____

2. 15 + 6 = ____

3. Circle the time.

5:00 12:00 5:30

4. If 17 + 4 = 21, then 21 − 4 = ____.

5. Mr. Brown asked 5 students to each bring 2 books they had read to the PTA meeting. How many books did they bring in all?

   ____ books

1. 9 + 5 = ____

2. 15 + 0 = ____

3. Write a number sentence.

____ ◯ ____ = ____

4. Six cars were parked in the first row. Seven cars were parked in the second row. Five cars were parked in the third row. Which row had the most cars?

   ◯ first ◯ second ◯ third

5. 8 > 6 ◯ **yes** ◯ **no**

➤ Activity 1

1. How many students like ice cream? _____ students
2. Which flavor do the students like best? ____________________
3. Do more students like butter pecan or vanilla? ____________________
4. Which flavor is your favorite? ____________________

➤ Activity 2

Write the missing numbers.

	2								10
							18		
			24						
									40

WEEK 29 DAY 1 Daily Math Practice

1 6 + 5 = _____

5 + 6 = _____

2 14 – 5 = _____

3 Sara's window has four corners and four equal sides. What shape is Sara's window?

○ triangle

○ square

○ rectangle

4 How much?

_____ cents

5 Circle the even numbers.

1 2 3 4 5 6 7 8

WEEK 29 DAY 2 Daily Math Practice

1 8 + 7 = _____

2

$$\begin{array}{r} 11 \\ +\ 3 \\ \hline \end{array} \qquad \begin{array}{r} 12 \\ +\ 2 \\ \hline \end{array}$$

3 Tessa has four brothers and two sisters. How many children are in Tessa's family?

_____ children

4 Which is longer?

○ one inch ○ one foot

5 Write a story for **7 – 5 = ?**

____

____

____

____

1 100 – 10 = _____

2 16 = _____ ten + _____ ones

40 = _____ tens + _____ ones

3 Carly sold three boxes of candy. Seth sold seven boxes. How many boxes did they sell altogether?

_____ boxes

4 Circle the shapes that have more than three sides.

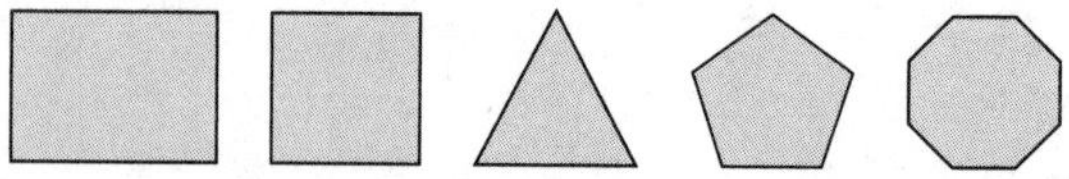

5

Add 10			
2		5	
3		6	
4		7	

1 19 + 10 = _____

2 20 + 40 + 10 = _____

3 If Tina has ten puppies and four leashes, how many puppies do **not** have leashes?

_____ puppies

4 Write four number sentences using **10**, **11**, and **21**.

_____ + _____ = _____

_____ + _____ = _____

_____ – _____ = _____

_____ – _____ = _____

5

$$\begin{array}{r} 8 \\ +\ 9 \\ \hline \end{array} \qquad \begin{array}{r} 9 \\ +\ 8 \\ \hline \end{array}$$

➤ Activity 1

Each student needs two pencils and a ruler to do a project. If there are six students, how many pencils do they need altogether?

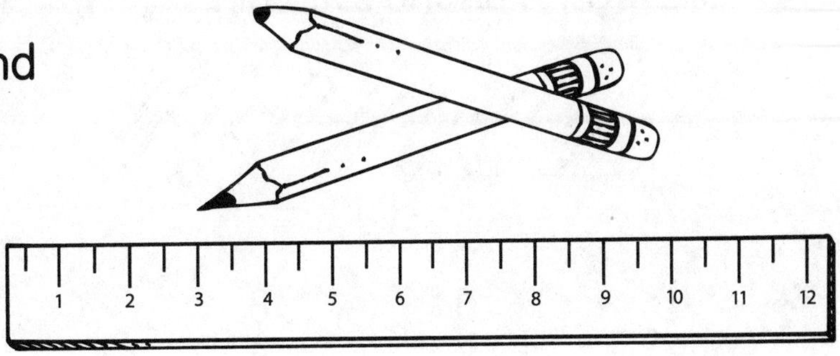

_____ pencils

How many rulers do they need altogether?

_____ rulers

Show your work.

➤ Activity 2

2 + 2 + 2 + 2 + 2 + 2 = _____

5 + 5 + 5 + 5 = _____

10 + 10 + 10 + 10 + 10 = _____

1 Draw an **X** on the sixth pin.

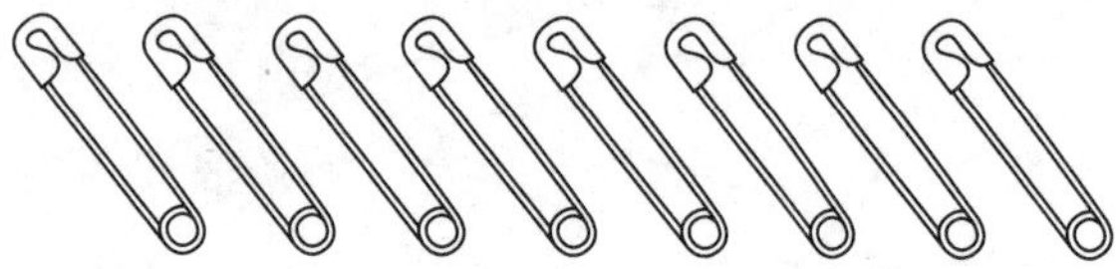

2

4	6	8
+ 8	+ 8	+ 8

3 How many letters are in Stephanie's name?

_____ letters

4 25 30 35 _____ _____

_____ _____ _____ _____

5 5 + 5 = _____

6 + 6 = _____

7 + 7 = _____

8 + 8 = _____

9 + 9 = _____

1 9 + 2 = _____

10 + 2 = _____

2 16 – 4 = _____

4 + _____ = 16

3 Eight coconuts were on the tree. Three fell off. How many are left?

_____ coconuts

4 Write the time.

_____ o'clock

5 Color the beads. Make the spheres green. Make the cubes purple.

1 17 − 8 = ____

2
```
  5     2
  5     2
+ 5   + 2
```

3 Minnie likes even numbers. Mickey likes odd numbers. Who likes **7**?

○ Minnie ○ Mickey

4 Write an addition number sentence.

____ + ____ + ____ = ____

5 Is 40 pounds heavier than 30 pounds?

○ **yes** ○ **no**

1 7 + 5 = 11 + 1 ○ **yes** ○ **no**

2 25 − 5 = ____

5 + ____ = 25

3 There are four plates, four cups, and four forks on the table. How many people can eat?

____ people

4 Show four ways to make **16**.

____ + ____ = 16

____ + ____ = 16

____ − ____ = 16

____ − ____ = 16

5 If 8 + 9 = 17,

then ____ = 9 + ____.

Activity 1

I put six pretzels, four candies, and two cookies in my snack bag. How many things do I have in all?

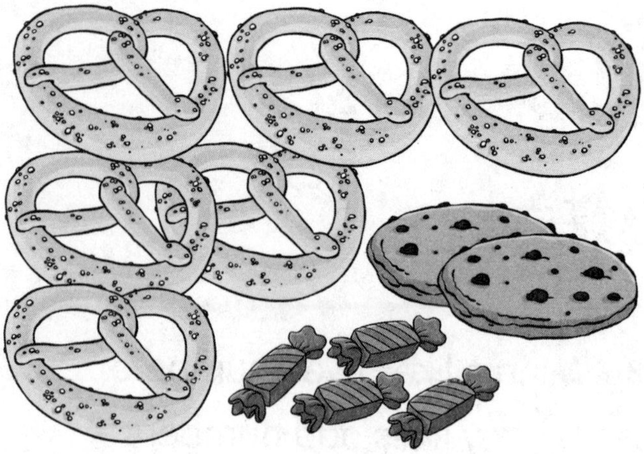

_____ things

If I eat the pretzels, how many things will I have left?

_____ things

Show your work.

Activity 2

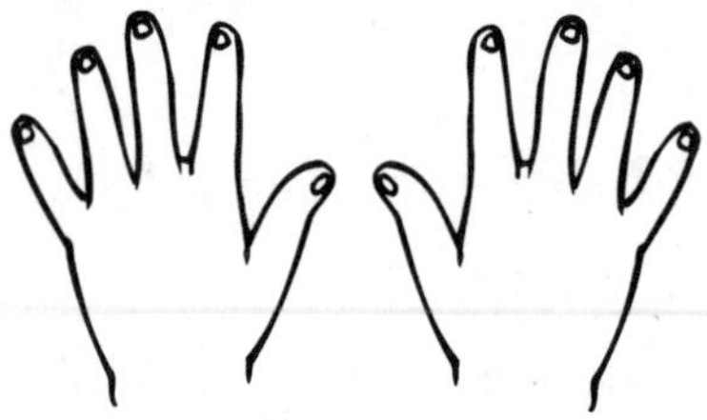

Circle the left hand.

Draw an **X** on the right hand.

1 6 + 4 = 7 + 3

○ yes

○ no

2 5 + 6 = _____

15 + 6 = _____

3 Tim had six paper clips. He used two on a puppet and two on a book. How many paper clips did he have left?

_____ paper clips

4 Color $\frac{1}{3}$ of all the pockets.

5 Match the words and numbers.

2	five three	5
3	six four	6
4	seven two	7

1

$$\begin{array}{r} 42 \\ -\ 2 \\ \hline \end{array} \qquad \begin{array}{r} 67 \\ -\ 5 \\ \hline \end{array}$$

2

$$\begin{array}{r} 341 \\ +\ 23 \\ \hline \end{array} \qquad \begin{array}{r} 404 \\ +\ 32 \\ \hline \end{array}$$

3 Seven bees flew to four flowers. How many more bees than flowers were there?

_____ more bees

4 About how many toothpicks?

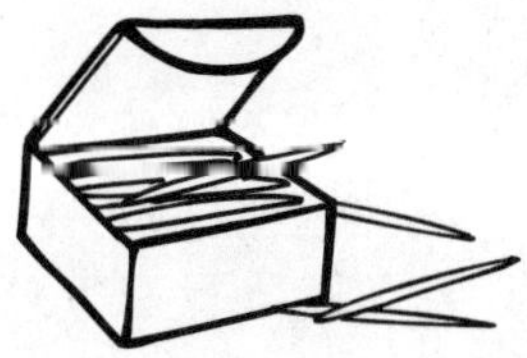

10 100 1,000

5 $9 < 9$ ○ yes ○ no

$9 > 9$ ○ yes ○ no

$9 = 9$ ○ yes ○ no

1 16 – 8 = ____

2 Match each shape to its name.

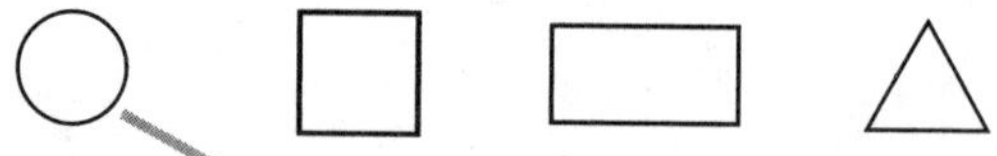

square circle triangle rectangle

3 Liz put six black beads and six brown beads on her necklace. How many beads did she use in all?

____ beads

4 Circle the ways to make **18**.

18 + 0 17 + 2 15 + 3

5 Three girls played jump rope. Four boys played tag. Six other children played four square. How many children played in all?

○ 3 + 4 = 7

○ 3 + 4 + 6 = 17

○ 3 + 4 + 6 = 13

1 Continue the pattern.

1 3 5 7 ____ ____ ____

2 4 + 7 + 2 = ____

3 Ava wants to fill a planter box. It holds five bags of soil. If Ava has two bags, how many more does she need?

____ more bags

4 15 – 5 = ____ 25 – 5 = ____

16 – 6 = ____ 26 – 6 = ____

17 – 7 = ____ 27 – 7 = ____

5 Are the sides the same?

○ **yes**

○ **no**

Activity 1

Show eight different ways to color the circles.

Use only red and blue. Plan before you color.

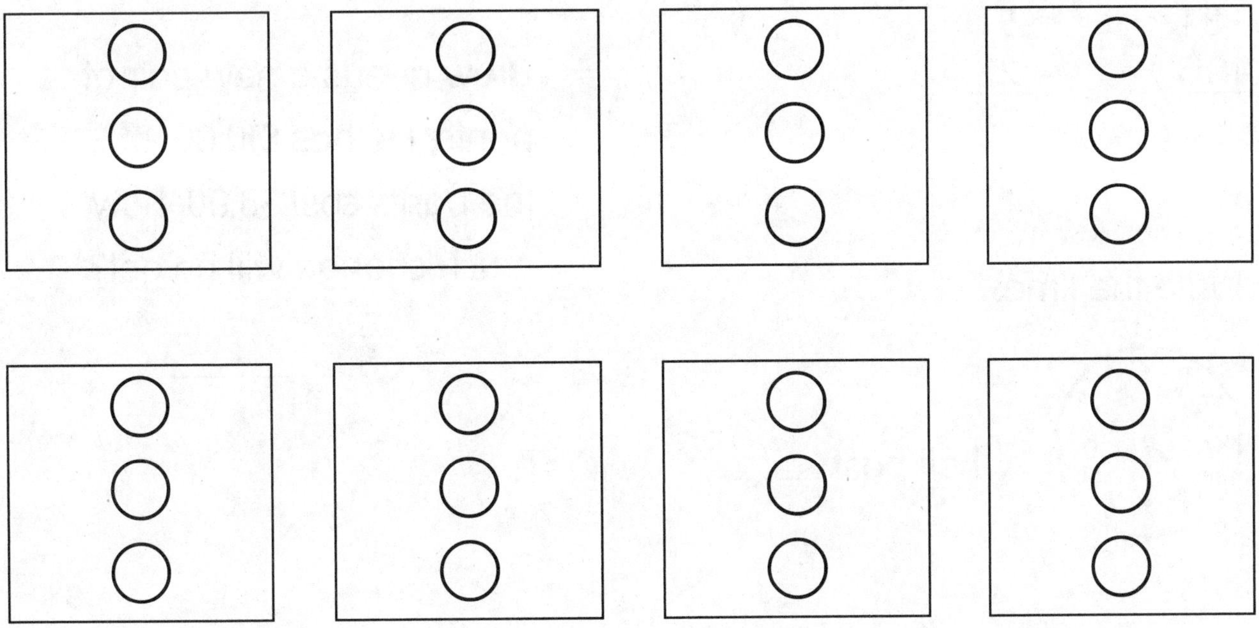

Activity 2

Rosa made a tower using four blocks as the base, three blocks for the next two levels, and one block on the top. How many blocks are in the tower?

_____ blocks

Draw the tower.

WEEK 32 DAY 1 Daily Math Practice

1 67 – 52 = _____

2

42	23
31	51
+15	+22

3 Write the time.

half past _____

4 If 54 + 32 = 86,

then _____ – 32 = _____.

5 Drew needs a new pair of pants. He has \$10.00. If the pants cost \$8.00, how much change will he get?

\$_________

WEEK 32 DAY 2 Daily Math Practice

1 4 + 2 + 7 + 1 = _____

2 5 + 3 – 2 = _____

3 Claire made a dozen cookies for her 6 friends. She will give the same number of cookies to each friend. How many will each friend get?

_____ cookies

4 Mark the name for the shaded part.

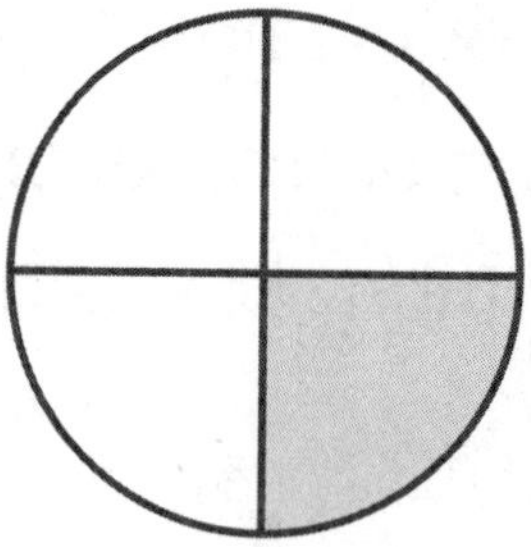

○ $\frac{1}{3}$

○ $\frac{2}{4}$

○ $\frac{1}{4}$

5 Write the number.

one hundred _____

1. 18 – 7 = _____

   7 + _____ = 18

2. 15 + 13 = _____

   28 – 15 = _____

3. 2 4 6 _____ _____ _____

   2 + 2 + 2 + 2 + 2 + 2 = _____

4. $647 < 532$ ○ **yes** ○ **no**

   $209 > 199$ ○ **yes** ○ **no**

5. Cindy has four nickels in her purse and two nickels in her pocket. How many nickels does she have in all?

   _____ nickels

   How much are they worth?

   _____¢

1. 3 + 4 + 9 = _____

2. 9 – 2 – 3 = _____

3. Color the rectangles.

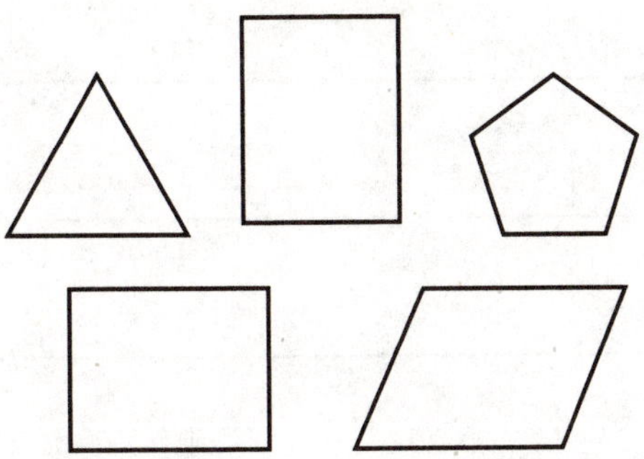

4. How many?

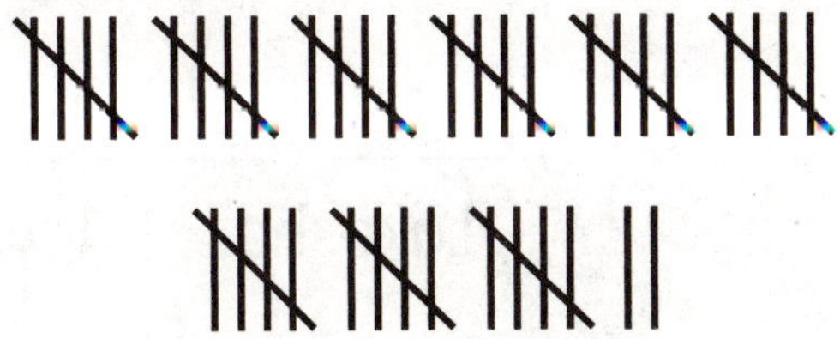

   _____ tally marks

5. Five frogs each ate five flies. How many flies did the frogs eat in all?

   _____ flies

1. Count the letters in each name: **Lakesha**, **Teyo**, **Emily**, **Ayden**, **Jon**. Color the boxes on the graph to show the number of letters for each name.

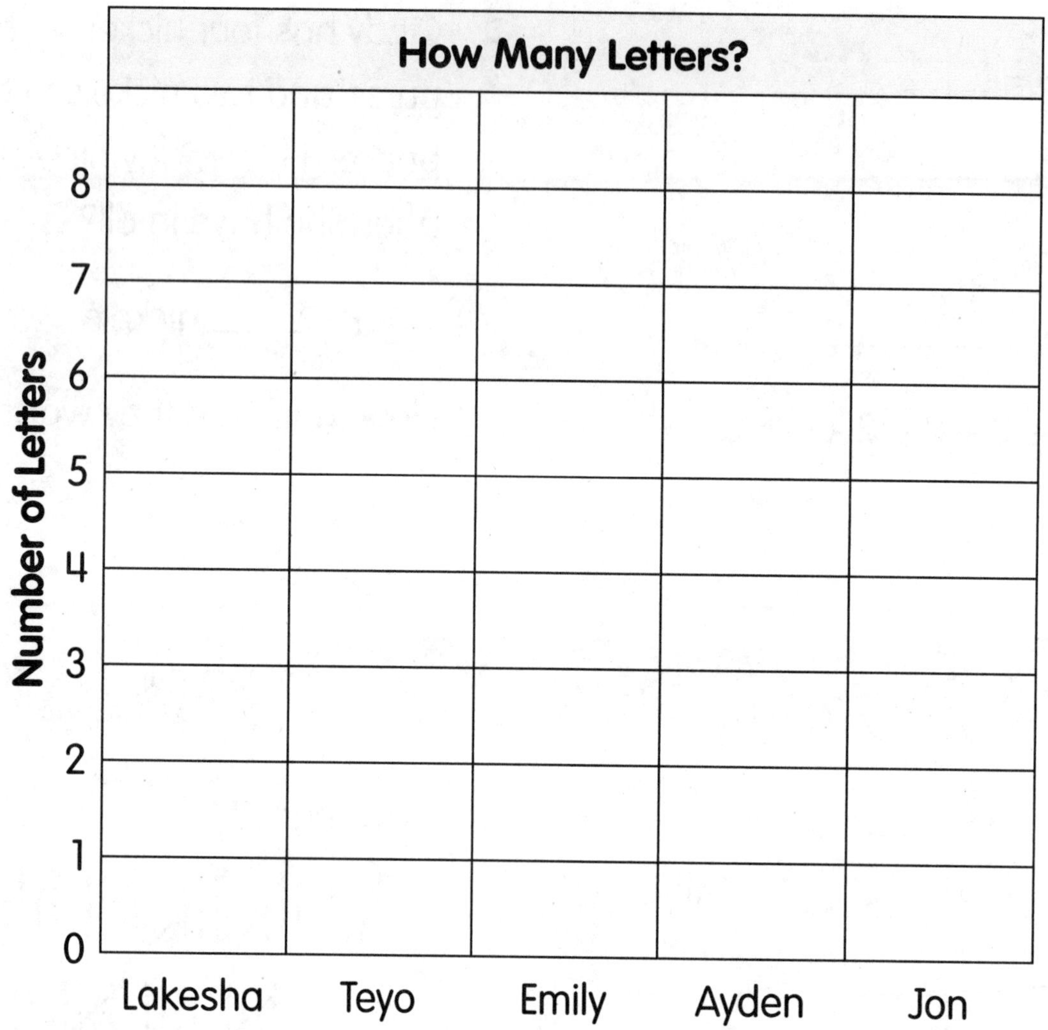

2. Write something you learned from the graph.

____

____

____

1 5 + 8 = ____

____ − 5 = 8

2 14 − 9 = ____

24 − 9 = ____

3 The fish tank has 6 guppies, 7 zebra fish, 1 catfish, and 1 snail. How many animals are in the fish tank?

____ animals

4 How much?

= ____ cents

= ____ cents

= ____ cents

5 6 + 2 + 1 + 0 = ____

1 17 − 7 = ____

17 − 8 = ____

17 − 9 = ____

2 14 + 6 = ____

3 50 60 70 ____ ____

____ ____ ____

4 Mark the pattern unit.

○ ABAC ○ ABAB ○ ABCA

5 The number is **73**.

How many tens? ____

How many ones? ____

1

$\begin{array}{r} 8 \\ -\ 2 \\ \hline \end{array}$ $\qquad$ $\begin{array}{r} 18 \\ -\ 2 \\ \hline \end{array}$

2

$\begin{array}{r} 7 \\ 1 \\ +\ 5 \\ \hline \end{array}$ $\qquad$ $\begin{array}{r} 8 \\ +\ 5 \\ \hline \end{array}$

3 Circle the ways to make **6**.

3 + 3	7 – 1	2 + 5
4 + 3	5 + 1	8 – 3

4 84 = _____ tens + _____ ones

70 = _____ tens + _____ ones

55 = _____ tens + _____ ones

5 Dave found four eggs in a nest and five eggs in a basket. How many eggs did he find in all?

_____ eggs

1 8 + 9 = _____

9 + 8 = _____

2 18 – 6 = _____

6 + _____ = 18

3 **32** is an odd number.

○ **yes** ○ **no**

4 Color the figures with four corners and four sides.

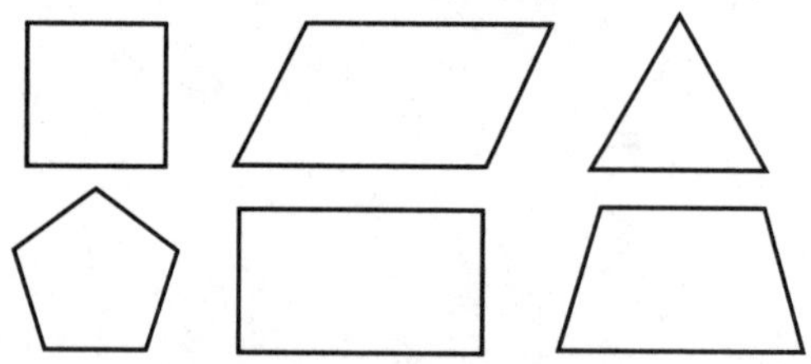

5 Mia and Jo each picked four flowers. They put three in a vase. How many flowers are left?

_____ flowers

Activity 1

Jesse cut out three hearts, six circles, and three squares.

He made an **ABBC** repeating pattern using all the shapes.

Draw **two** patterns he could have made.

Activity 2

Draw an **ABCB** repeating pattern. Use triangles, rectangles, and circles.

1

52	74
−41	− 23

2

37	85
+41	+ 12

3 Erik ate five pieces of pizza. If the pizza was cut into eight pieces, how many are left?

_____ pieces

4 Draw an **X** on the tenth banana.

5 10 + 2 = ?

Circle the correct answers.

4 + 8

11 + 0

9 + 3

1 Two pounds > $\frac{1}{2}$ pound.

○ **yes** ○ **no**

2

73	51
14	23
+12	+ 15

3 5 10 15 _____ _____ _____

_____ _____ _____ _____

4 Circle the clock that shows half past six.

5 Six kids each make two piles of sand. How many piles of sand are there in all?

_____ piles

WEEK 34 DAY 3 Daily Math Practice

1 943 – 10 = _____

2 Circle the even numbers.

3 8 1 6 4 2 9

3 7 + 10 = _____

6 + 10 = _____

7 + 100 = _____

6 + 100 = _____

4 Twenty-six first graders are going to the dairy. A bus holds fourteen students. How many buses will they need?

_____ buses

How many extra seats will there be?

_____ seats

5 seven 

s = _____ cents

WEEK 34 DAY 4 Daily Math Practice

1 8 + 2 + 5 + 3 = _____

2 If 25 + 34 = 59,

then _____ – 34 = _____.

3 9 – 9 = _____

8 – 8 = _____

7 – 7 = _____

6 – 6 = _____

4 Ronni rode her bike 8 blocks to Joe's house and back home. How many blocks did Ronni ride by the time she got home?

_____ blocks

5 Write a number sentence to show how many legs there are.

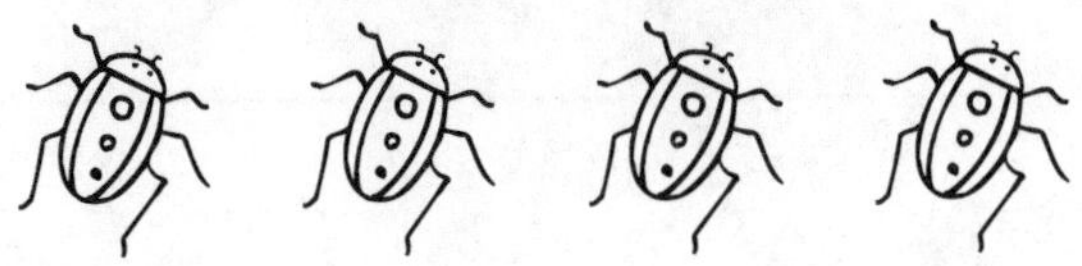

_____ + _____ + _____ + _____ = _____

1. Look at the data. Color one square on the graph for each book.

Data	
animal books	卌 |||
fairy tales	卌 ||
sports books	||
chapter books	||||
holiday books	卌

The Books We Read

animal										
fairy tales										
sports										
chapter										
holiday										

0 1 2 3 4 5 6 7 8 9 10

2. Look at the graph and write something you learned.

____

____

____

1 4 + 5 + 3 + 0 = ____

2 Are the two parts the same?

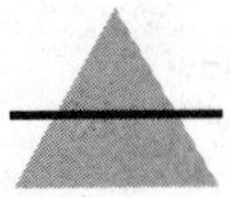

○ **yes** ○ **no**

3 If Daren pops three balloons, how many balloons will be left?

____ balloons

4 11 + 10 = ____

12 + 10 = ____

13 + 10 = ____

14 + 10 = ____

15 + 10 = ____

5 10 20 30 ____ ____

____ ____ ____ ____

____ ____ ____ ____

1 17 – 8 = ____

2 8 + 1 + 4 = ____

3 At the movies, 4 children are in the fourth row, 3 in the third row, 2 in the second row, and 1 in the first row. How many children are there in all?

____ children

4 If 64 – 33 = 31,

then ____ – 31 = ____.

5 Write an addition number sentence.

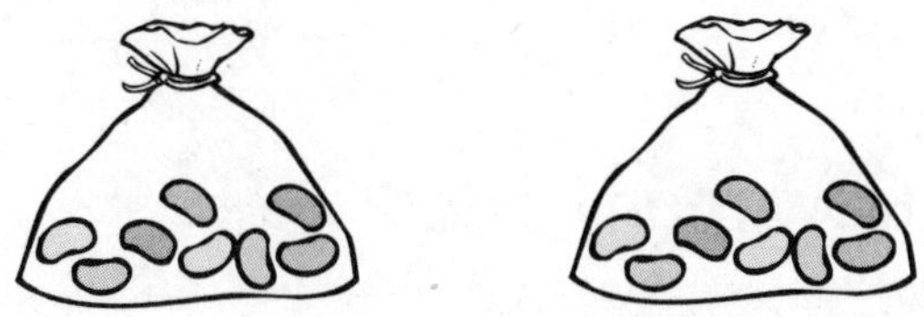

____ ○ ____ ○ ____

WEEK 35 DAY 3 Daily Math Practice

1 $5 + 2 + 7 =$ ____

2 $8 - 4 =$ ____

$38 - 34 =$ ____

3 At the game, Alec made 4 goals. He scored two points for each goal. How many points did he score in all?

____ points

4 Continue the pattern.

○ ○ □ ○ ○ □ ○

____ ____

5 About how many marshmallows?

more than 20 less than 20

WEEK 35 DAY 4 Daily Math Practice

1 $62 + 37 =$ ____

$37 + 62 =$ ____

2 $19 - 8 =$ ____

$19 - 9 =$ ____

3 How many sides?

one square = ____ sides

two squares = ____ sides

4 90 80 70 ____ ____ ____

____ ____ ____ ____

5 Michael is 48 inches tall. Sandi is 2 inches taller than Michael. How many inches tall is Sandi?

____ inches

Activity 1

Look at the grid. Show how to find each animal. Begin at the star.

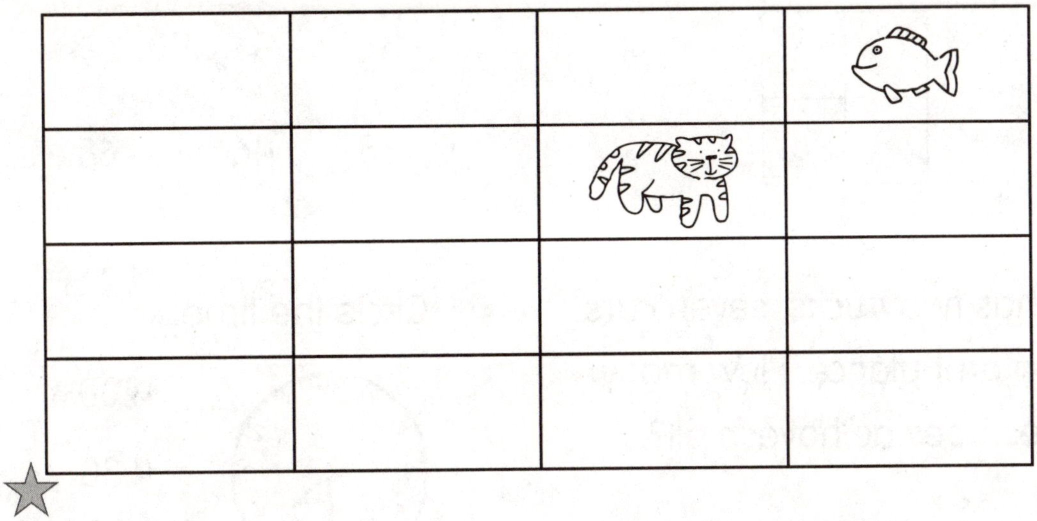

1.  over ____

   up ____

2.  over ____

   up ____

Activity 2

Color the numbers to count by fives.

1	2	3	4	5	6	7	8	9	10
11	12	13	14	15	16	17	18	19	20
21	22	23	24	25	26	27	28	29	30
31	32	33	34	35	36	37	38	39	40
41	42	43	44	45	46	47	48	49	50
51	52	53	54	55	56	57	58	59	60
61	62	63	64	65	66	67	68	69	70
71	72	73	74	75	76	77	78	79	80
81	82	83	84	85	86	87	88	89	90
91	92	93	94	95	96	97	98	99	100

1. 325 – 214 = ______

2. Color $\frac{1}{4}$.

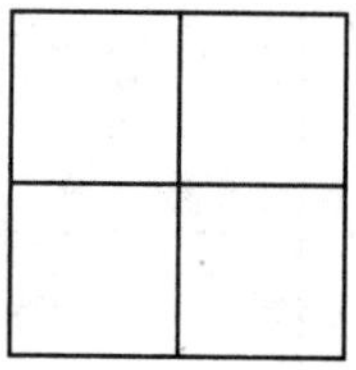

3. Sabir has two trucks, seven cars, and an ambulance. How many vehicles does he have in all?

 ______ vehicles

4. Write the correct symbol in the circle.

< = >

38 ◯ 46   68 ◯ 79

5. Circle the time.

4:00

4:30

6:00

1. 47 + 22 = ______

2.

$$\begin{array}{r} 5 \\ 10 \\ 4 \\ +10 \\ \hline \end{array} \qquad \begin{array}{r} 15 \\ +14 \\ \hline \end{array}$$

3. Continue the pattern.

21 + 0   22 + 0   23 + 0

________ ________

4. How many?

 ______ tally marks

5. There are twenty parking spaces in the lot. Fifteen cars are parked. How many spaces are empty?

 ______ spaces

WEEK 36 DAY 3 — Daily Math Practice

1. 89 – 34 = ____

2. 73 + 15 = ____

3. Seven friends went to the store. They each had two dollars to spend. How much money did they have altogether?

   $________

4. Count by 2s.

   72 ____ 76 ____ 80 ____

   84 ____ 88 ____

5. Write the number.

   forty-one ____

   forty-four ____

   forty-nine ____

   fifty-two ____

WEEK 36 DAY 4 — Daily Math Practice

1. 24 + 43 = ____

2. 38 – 6 = ____

3. Joy has seven eggs. How many more eggs does she need to fill the carton?

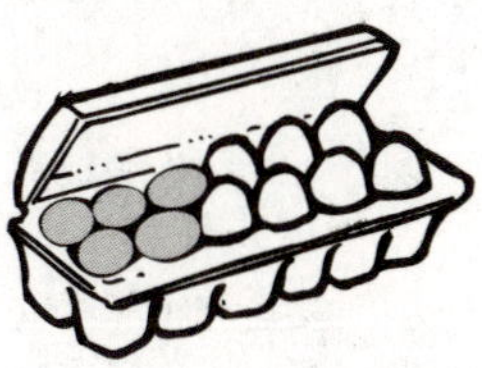

   ____ eggs

4. Continue the pattern.

   △ ▽ △ ▽ ____

   ____ ____ ____

5. Circle the clock that shows the same time.

   6:00

   12:00

   12:30

1. Josh wanted to sort his Legos®. Think about how he could sort them into two groups.

2. Draw to show which shapes would go in each group. Then write the rule.

Group 1	Group 2
This group ________________.	This group ________________.

How to Solve

Word Problems

- Read the problem carefully. Think about what it says.
- Read the problem again and look for clue words. They will tell you which operation to use. Below are some examples of clue words.
- Solve the problem. **Hint:** Sometimes you will use more than one operation.
- Check your work. Does your answer make sense?

Clue Words

Add		Subtract	
total	sum	less than	fewer
in all	plus	more than	are left
altogether	both	take away	difference

100 Chart

1	2	3	4	5	6	7	8	9	10
11	12	13	14	15	16	17	18	19	20
21	22	23	24	25	26	27	28	29	30
31	32	33	34	35	36	37	38	39	40
41	42	43	44	45	46	47	48	49	50
51	52	53	54	55	56	57	58	59	60
61	62	63	64	65	66	67	68	69	70
71	72	73	74	75	76	77	78	79	80
81	82	83	84	85	86	87	88	89	90
91	92	93	94	95	96	97	98	99	100

Congratulations!

____
(name)

You have successfully completed your math practice!